Bereavement

ISSUES
(formerly Issues for the Nineties)

Volume 41

Editor

Craig Donnellan

Independence
Educational Publishers
Cambridge

First published by Independence
PO Box 295
Cambridge CB1 3XP
England

British Library Cataloguing in Publication Data
Bereavement – (Issues Series)
I. Donnellan, Craig II. Series
155.9'37

ISBN 1 86168 083 X

Printed in Great Britain
City Print Ltd
Milton Keynes

Typeset by
Claire Boyd

Cover
The illustration on the front cover is by
Pumpkin House.

CONTENTS

Introduction

Bereavement is the forty-first volume in the series: **Issues**. The aim of this series is to offer up-to-date information about important issues in our world.

Bereavement looks at the ways we cope with death.

The information comes from a wide variety of sources and includes:
Government reports and statistics
Newspaper reports and features
Magazine articles and surveys
Literature from lobby groups
and charitable organisations.

It is hoped that, as you read about the many aspects of the issues explored in this book, you will critically evaluate the information presented. It is important that you decide whether you are being presented with facts or opinions. Does the writer give a biased or an unbiased report? If an opinion is being expressed, do you agree with the writer?

Bereavement offers a useful starting-point for those who need convenient access to information about the many issues involved. However, it is only a starting-point. At the back of the book is a list of organisations which you may want to contact for further information.

*****

Coping with bereavement

There is no right way to cope when someone you know has died

How you feel, think and behave may differ from anyone else. People from different communities will have their own ways of responding. Nevertheless, you might find yourself reacting in some of the ways that are described in this article.

Numbness and shock

It is very common to feel shocked at first, especially if the death was unexpected for you. You could feel completely numb, even though it might seem wrong not to be overcome with grief. This numbness may be helpful if you have tasks to perform such as registering the death or arranging the funeral.

Disbelief

Disbelief is also a common reaction, being unable to accept that the one you love will not be there any more. It may take a long time for the fact of their death to sink in. In the meantime you may behave in some ways as though they are still alive. One example may be setting their place at the table for meals, forgetting they will never come home again.

Searching

Your yearning for the person you care about could be very intense. You may even find yourself searching for them, in the street or wherever you go, perhaps recognising the back of their head, or seeing them going into a shop, only to find that it is a complete stranger.

Grief

The pain of grief can seem unbearable when it occurs. You may find that you want to cry all the time. Or there may be no tears, despite your sorrow. People may tell you that 'time heals', that you will feel better eventually, yet in your experience the grief may go on without lessening. It is hard to believe that you can ever come to terms with such a loss.

Stress and physical symptoms

It is not unusual to experience stress, or to have headaches, palpitations, dizziness or diarrhoea. You may also suffer from a tightness in the chest, aches and pains, tiredness and loss of appetite. You may want to sleep a great deal, or be unable to stop yawning. These symptoms are all normal, but it may help to talk to your doctor about anything which worries you.

Fear

Perhaps there will be feelings of great fear, even panic. You may fear that you will die too, or that other people you care about may be going to die soon. It is possible that you will have bad dreams and disturbed sleep, and a confusion of different feelings that are hard to cope with. Alongside that there may be a lot of frightening thoughts about death.

Anger

It is perfectly normal to feel angry after a death, especially of someone close. The intensity of rage may take some people by surprise. Anger may be directed at the dead person, for dying and leaving you. You may be angry at other people, because their lives are unaffected, or they seem insensitive, or because you feel they are to blame. You might also be very angry with yourself for all sorts of reasons, including guilt.

Guilt

People often feel a lot of guilt after someone dies, perhaps blaming themselves. They may think that they could have been more caring to the deceased when he or she was alive. This could lead to feelings of regret, thinking of how things might have happened differently. None of us conduct our relationships as though we will never see someone again, so there might easily be reasons for such guilt. Sometimes just the fact of still being alive can lead to guilty feelings.

Relief

Another reaction to death may be a sense of relief. You may feel relieved that now the person you care about is beyond pain. Perhaps it was a great strain on you, knowing someone who was suffering, and you felt that you had no right to your feelings of resentment or sadness when someone close to you was dying of AIDS. It may be that the person who died really was difficult to get along with sometimes, or felt like a burden on you. To have such feelings is perfectly normal. It doesn't mean you are a bad person. Alongside this you may still have other emotions like anger or grief.

Despair and suicidal feelings

There may be a total sense of despair, a feeling that life is no longer worth living. It may seem that nothing and no one else matters – which can be devastating to our relationship with people who are still alive. It's not unusual to feel like this now, but these desperate feelings will lessen with time.

The feelings of the bereaved often have a lot in common with depression. It may seem as if life has no meaning. You may want to stay at home and see no one. It may be hard to look after yourself properly, to put on clean clothes or to bother with food or washing up. These are natural ways to react, but if they go on too long they might become a problem, and then may be a time to seek help.

Overwork, shopping, drink, drugs, sex or food can all be things we turn to when we are unhappy. We may do anything to avoid the pain of loss. For some people, the best way not to be aware of their grief or anger may be to plunge into their work, so that there is no time to think. Others may find themselves spending more money than they can afford. Still others may find that they are drinking alcohol, or eating, or using drugs, to excess.

Some people may turn to frequent sex with many different partners. At the same time you may be feeling a disregard for the value of your life, and perhaps drinking a lot or using drugs. You may also find that you are having unprotected sex. Even if you are not, you may feel that

this aspect of your life is out of your control, and that you are un-comfortable with how you are behaving.

If you feel concerned about any of these things, this may be a time to look for help or support from someone such as a counsellor, who can listen to you non-judgmentally. If you do not want to see someone face to face, there are a number of telephone helplines to choose from.

Looking after yourself

It is important to keep looking after yourself at this time. This might mean getting enough sleep, washing regularly, dressing in clean clothes, or giving yourself little treats. It may also mean not having an extra drink or an extra portion of food, if these things are causing you concern.

The grieving process

We need to give ourselves time to mourn. At the beginning of this process there is often disbelief, rage and a lot of grief. These feelings may seem to continue without lessening, but in time there will be changes. It may be a very slow process. Major decisions, about moving house or leaving your job, are not necessarily a good idea to begin with. There is often a need to talk, to share your memories of the deceased. If you can find someone you feel comfortable talking to about these things, this can be helpful, even though it will not bring back the person you love.

Saying goodbye

As part of the grieving process it may be important to find ways to say goodbye to the person who has died. Viewing the body may be a way of doing this. In some cultures it is the custom to hold a vigil beside the body for a week after death. You may find that going to the funeral can

help in the process of saying goodbye, or you might choose to hold a memorial or thanksgiving service later on. These rituals could take a traditional form, conducted by a priest or religious leader, or you might want to design your own form of service, with the help of friends or family. For example, you may want to play a choice of music, choose poems to read, and invite people to speak.

Attending the body or visiting the grave may not be possible for you if someone important to you has died in another country, such as in Africa, especially if there are reasons why you cannot visit there. Some employers or friends may not understand the importance of a week-long vigil, and it is hard to have to give explanations at such a time.

Spiritual help

Some people are part of a religious community where they can find support. Others may have their own spiritual practice which they can turn to. Often, people find themselves looking for some way of responding to their loss that cannot be met by friends or counsellors. Perhaps you may find yourself saying prayers or talking to God for the first time in years. It may be helpful to speak to a spiritual leader. Just sitting quietly in a peaceful garden, or going for a walk by the sea, may offer you something which you cannot get anywhere else at this time.

Dealing with more than one death

Even one death can feel like too much to bear. It may often be much worse when you lose two or more people. Some people have had to face the wiping out of virtually their entire network of friends or family during the AIDS epidemic. For many people this loss of life is still continuing on a wide scale. For people in African communities, multiple bereavement can be harder to deal with because you are far away from your family or friends.

After the death of a number of people whom you care about, you may be feeling a huge emptiness in your life. You may be overcome by suicidal feelings, or have panic attacks, or find that you can't shake off thoughts about death and dying. You may lose all hope, have no interest in the possibility of a cure for AIDS, and avoid all possibility of getting close to anyone. You could find that you are drinking or using drugs more than you used to, or having sex a lot more, and feeling that your life is out of control. None of these things is unusual under the circumstances. If you feel overwhelmed or very depressed, however, this could be the time to find help from a professional counsellor or support group.

'There's no one I can talk to' – AIDS and secrecy

Sometimes it can seem as though there is no one to turn to. It may be that the people you work with, or your friends and neighbours, have no inkling that you have lost someone through AIDS. You may be afraid of them finding out, in case they are prejudiced, or you fear they might discriminate against you, or ostracise you. Or it may be that people you feel close to are unable to bear hearing about your grief, perhaps because they feel uncomfortable about AIDS and death. Not being able to talk about some of your feelings, or keeping things secret, can make the grief much harder to bear. This may be a good time to think about seeking support from an organisation.

Losing a partner

The death of a partner, especially if you were together for a long time, can leave a big space in your life. There is no longer anyone there to share things with as you used to. Their physical absence is particularly noticeable if you shared a bed. In some communities it is normal to go into mourning for a year. This can have a beneficial aspect, as it offers a structure within which your bereavement can be recognised. But it can be difficult if the mourning period is not respected by others, because they do not share your customs.

It can be very painful coming to terms with your new identity as a single person. For any bereaved partner, social occasions can be difficult to deal with, and remind you of your loss. And what should you do if you are invited out by another person? Is that a betrayal of your partner, even if there is no romantic intention? Is it OK to have a new relationship, or even a casual encounter? These questions may take a while to answer. It is important not to give yourself a hard time as you chart this new territory. Take it slowly, and don't feel that you have to do anything.

Death of a same-sex partner

When someone's husband or wife dies, there's a new role of widow or widower. The surviving partner has a certain status, with legal and social rights. Without these, your grief may not feel acceptable – in the workplace, for example. And if the diagnosis of AIDS was not public knowledge, or the fact that you were in a gay relationship, this element of secrecy can increase your sense of isolation and make the loss much harder to deal with. As with any surviving partner, there may be questions about your own HIV status. If your partner did not leave a will, there may be problems about property, and who is the legal heir. In some cases you may be forced to move house. If necessary you should seek legal advice, e.g. from The Terrence Higgins Trust. The Lesbian and Gay Bereavement Project can also offer support and advice.

Living with HIV

If you are HIV positive yourself, the death of someone you know may have a powerful impact. Questions about your own health could come up, and increased anxiety about the future. There might be feelings of guilt because you are still alive, for some people. Because it can be a difficult time for people with HIV, it is especially important to look after yourself now. Remember that help and support are available to you if you want them. PositiveLine is run by people who are themselves HIV positive. Other helplines can tell you how to get support near where you live, like The Terrence Higgins Trust helpline, or Blackliners.

Death of a son or daughter

If you are a parent who has lost a son or daughter, having to come to terms with the death of your own child can seem especially unfair and hard to bear. Children are usually expected to outlive their parents. In your darker moments, you may even feel some guilt or responsibility for your child's death. Nagging thoughts may tell you that you could have done things differently in the past. It can be helpful to remember that as a parent you probably did the best that you could, all things considered. It is important to remember the good times you had together. It may help to think about the things you especially loved about your child, and her or his unique contribution to the world. Try to be easy on yourself and not to blame yourself for anyone's death. The Compassionate Friends is an organisation which offers support to bereaved parents, and it is run by people who have themselves lost a son or daughter. They can also help people who are grieving for a sister or brother.

Children need to grieve too. If a family member or a family friend has died, it is important to include children in what is happening. If there are discussions about the deceased, or rituals taking place, such as a funeral service, it is good to try to find ways that they can join in, if they wish. As with adults, they may need to talk and share memories, good and bad, about the person they've lost. Tell them the truth about what has happened, and answer any questions they may have. Use language and ideas that they can understand, but avoid any pretence that someone 'has gone away for a while'.

Children are unique, and will have their own ways of grieving. Sometimes they may seem very matter of fact. They may make surprisingly forthright remarks. They may revert to being as they were when younger. A child may start sucking her thumb again, or an older child may want to sit on your lap as he did when little. Do not discourage them from such behaviour – in time, and with help, they will find ways of coming to terms with the loss, and 'grow up' again. There are many books available that can help children understand about death. Cruse and The Compassionate Friends can send you books through the post.

Practical arrangements

When someone dies there are always a number of practical tasks that need to be done. Their doctor must be notified, the death needs to be registered, and burial or cremation needs to be arranged. This may be more complex if the body needs to be shipped back to another country. In addition there may be everyday matters such as taking care of pets, making sure the home is secure, etc. In time there will be further tasks to be taken care of, such as dealing with property, and bank accounts. There may be immigration issues, if your status as a British resident depends on a partner who has died. You can get advice from The Terrence Higgins Trust, which has a helpline and a legal service you can contact.

The future

In time, it is likely that the pain of bereavement will decrease, although this may happen very slowly. Part of the process of moving on may be in accepting that the person is really dead. Although your life will never be the same, after a while you will begin to notice that you are not always sad or angry. There will still be difficult times, for example on anniversaries or birthdays. Perhaps you may feel guilty that you are able to take pleasure in life again. There may also be a fear that you will forget the person you cared about. But it is likely that you will begin to recall some of your happier memories of the deceased, and the times you spent together. Losing someone because of AIDS must always be a tragic event,

and nothing can compensate for this loss. However, you may find that something worthwhile can come out of a terrible experience, and that you have changed for the better in some ways, or gained something valuable you didn't have before.

Supporting someone who has been bereaved

If someone you know has recently lost someone because of AIDS, you may want to help and support them. Friends are important at such a time. To begin with, the person is likely to be dazed or preoccupied. Practical support is useful. The person may need help in arranging a funeral, or organising everyday life. They may appreciate help with ordinary tasks such as doing the shopping, cooking meals or taking care of children. Check first what help they need, don't take control of their lives.

On the other hand, they may want you just to be around. It is not a good idea to cheer the person up. Just be there and listen, if they want to talk, without making demands.

Expressing your feelings may help them too, but don't burden them with your own grief, or force them to talk about their own feelings unless they want to. It is more hurtful not to mention the dead person, and in trying to spare their feelings you could make them feel that they can't talk to you.

Grief is a slow process. People need time to heal or adapt. Don't give advice, as the bereaved person needs to find their own way. If you feel that they are having difficulty in coming to terms with their loss, then you may suggest they find a counsellor. Check that this is what they want, as it is important not to force them or tell them they ought to seek help.

Further help

The Terrence Higgins Trust
52-54 Grays Inn Road, London, WC1X 8JU.Tel: 0171 831 0330 – Administration, 0171 242 1010 – Helpline, 0171 405 2381 – Legal Line
The Terrence Higgins Trust offers a wide range of free and confidential services.

Counselling is available for anyone affected by or concerned about HIV. This includes individuals, couples, families and groups of friends. You will always be seen by a trained counsellor or therapist with a good knowledge of HIV and bereave-ment issues.

To access any of these services, please telephone us on 0171 831 0330.

Grieving

How can we help?

How to help someone who is grieving

The following articles, written by bereavement counsellors in the United States, contain information and advice which we believe you might find useful if you are helping a friend who is grieving – or indeed, if you are bereaved yourself and trying to get to grips with your own loss.

Being a supportive friend to a grieving person

Be aware: Grief is a natural and necessary process.

Be there: Grief is not a problem to be solved, but a process to be experienced.

Be sensitive: Learn to allow the pain rather than to remove it.

Be human: Allow expression of feelings – guilt, anger, sorrow, depression – without judgement.

Be ready: Listen attentively when the story is told again and again.

Be patient: The process of mourning takes time.

When a person is grieving and we do not know the right thing to say or do, we may end up doing nothing. The following are some specific suggestions to consider when helping a grieving person.

Common mistakes

'Don't take it so hard'

It only makes a bereaved person feel worse to hear, 'Be strong: don't take it so hard.' This sounds as though the loss is insignificant and deprives the person of the natural emotions of grief. Taking an honest attitude of 'I know this is tough to go through' gives the bereaved a chance to express and thus recover from grief.

The diversionary tactic

Many people calling on the bereaved purposely veer away from the subject of death and talk about football, fishing, the weather – anything but the reason for their call or visit. This attempt to camouflage death ignores the task of the mourner – facing the fact of death and going on from there. It would be far better to sit silently and say nothing than to make obvious attempts to distract. The grieving person can see through efforts to divert and reality hits all the harder when the diversion is absent.

'Let's not talk about it'

Well-meaning people often use this method of not mentioning the deceased, but the implication is the subject is too terrible to discuss politely. It is more helpful to evoke memories of the deceased in the fullness of life and to recreate a living picture to replace the picture of death.

'I don't want to make you cry'

Tears are a healthy expression of grief. Helping someone cry, being there with a shoulder to cry on is one of the most healing things one person can do for another. The repression of grief hampers growth.

Easy aides

Listen

Grieving people need to talk. Rather than worry about saying the right thing, concentrate upon warm, non-judgmental listening. Though the bereaved may want to repeat the same things a dozen times, these feelings need repetition to be dispelled. If the grieving person has said one hundred words to the listener's one, then the listener has helped.

Reach out – keep in touch

A person who has lost a loved one is often overwhelmed with visitors for a week or two; then the house is empty. Even good friends stay away, believing people in sorrow like to be alone. This is the silent treatment: to the bereaved person, it feels like abandonment, and there is nothing worse. Not only is the bereaved feeling the loss of the loved one, but of friends as well. Friends, people who will listen non-judgmentally, are needed most when all of the sympathy letters have been read and acknowledged and when others have gone back to their daily routines. Someone being there for the bereaved is proof of continued meaning and purpose in life.

Do something real

Small things make a big difference in showing someone you care. One tangible and practical act of kindness – running an errand, taking children to school, bringing in a meal, picking up the mail, helping to acknowledge notes – can make an immense impact on the well-being of the bereaved.

Help build a bridge to the future

People in grief often withdraw. Help build a bridge to the future: encourage a renewal of past activities and hobbies, offer rides to meetings, be a gentle reminder of activities enjoyed in the past.

Encourage new beginnings

Grief will run its natural course. Avoiding the trap of self-pity sometimes can be accomplished by taking up a new activity or pursuing a new interest. Grief is resolved when the bereaved becomes self-reliant and begins doing things for others.

This article, along with similar self-help information and links, can be found on the Hospice Hands site (www.hospice-cares.com/friends. hmtl).

North Central Florida Hospice, Inc. 1996

Helping families cope with death and dying

What to say

When caring for someone who's lost a loved one, specific questions and phrases can help them express their feelings:

I'm sorry for your loss.

Tell me how you're feeling.

Were you there when (name of loved one) died?

What was that like for you?

Tell me about (name of loved one) and your life with her.

What special memories do you have?

Keep in mind that you don't always have to say something. Sometimes your presence alone can be just as therapeutic as verbal communication. Crying with the family member and touching him on the hand, arm, shoulder, or back is also acceptable, when appropriate, and shows your compassion.

On the other hand, don't say things just to make yourself feel better or more comfortable around the bereaved. And avoid using clichés and other common phrases that may not be true or appropriate:

I know just how you feel.

Her death was for the best.

Things will get better.

Time heals all wounds.

Now you have an angel in heaven watching over you.

(From *Nursing*, July 96)

1996-1998 by Springhouse Corporation.

• This collection of articles appeared on the web site of The Prince & Princess of Wales Hospice: www. ppwh.org.uk

© *The Prince & Princess of Wales Hospice*

Drawn to the light

When Christine Longaker lost her husband to leukaemia, the pain of bereavement was unbearable. That grief led her to search for ways of coping and coming to terms with death. Now, as Duncan Campbell reports, she has written a poignant book on her 'spiritual journey'

In 1976, Christine Longaker's husband, Lyttle, was diagnosed with acute leukaemia at the age of 24 and died the following year. Now, more than 20 years later, she has written a remarkable book (published this month) about death and dying which has its origins in what she learned during the fatal illness of her husband.

Already translated into eight languages, *Facing Death and Finding Hope: A Guide to the Emotional and Spiritual Care of the Dying* is the result of not only her own personal experience but a compilation of what she learned during her years working in the hospice movement in the United States, embarking on her own 'spiritual path' as she describes it, and studying the literature on death and dying from a variety of sources, some religious, some not.

When Christine's husband, a radiology technician, contracted leukaemia, she was working for a mail order company and bringing up their young son, Donovan, in Santa Monica, California. Although she says she learned much from Lyttle's last year, she found her subsequent bereavement 'unbearable'. Her book is an attempt to explain how any of us can deal with death and dying in a more hopeful way, whether we are facing death ourselves or are family, friends or people working with the dying.

It is worth saying early on that she has used her knowledge of Tibetan Buddhist teachings on the 'art' or 'science of dying' to explain a spiritual dimension of living and dying but the book gives examples from other traditions, including Christian and Jewish, and does not suggest that the adoption of any faith is a prerequisite for trying to understand or prepare well for death.

'Sometimes if people hear the words "spiritual care" they think it's about converting the person, so I try to reassure people that it is not,' she says. 'But I have learned that many people have an intuitive feeling about the spiritual dimension of living and dying yet they don't know what to do with it if they're not following a formal religion.'

She is wary, too, of the platitudinous approach to death, the notion that there can be a swift, handy guide to such a complex process: 'This is not a "how-to" book. There isn't a right way to die. I think what a person who is dying needs is support in their own journey, whatever that is, and the most vital support is our human connection with them. Once we break down any barrier of fear or judgment and realise that we are two human beings who are both on a journey towards death, we can invite the dying to share with us what they are learning, and accompany them.'

The book itself deals with many of the diverse challenges that death poses: understanding children's views of death, surviving a suicide or sudden death, grief as experienced by adolescents whose peers feel uncomfortable with it, relating to those suffering from dementia or in a coma.

So where does she stand on one of the current key debates about dying – euthanasia?

'Unfortunately, a side-effect of the lack of awareness of the hospice movement is that people see dying as a state of helplessness, a lack of dignity and respect, a state of unmitigated grief and meaningless suffering and then they think euthanasia is a good idea because it seems to relieve all those problems. But hospices are designed to recognise and address all of these fears, and it's the best form of care we can give to the dying, whether they have cancer or heart disease or dementia or whatever the problem. So we now know how to relieve the various pains of dying, and the real debate should be about making hospice care available for all.'

She is an impassioned supporter of the hospice movement – there were four in the US when her husband died, there are now more than 2,000 – and is puzzled that governments do not realise that not only do hospices benefit the terminally ill and their families and friends but they are cheaper than the costly technology of life-support

machines. She is critical of the fact that most doctors get little or no training in palliative care and handling pain in terminal illness, as this results in much unnecessary suffering.

She encourages us to empathise with the friend or relative who is dying rather than viewing them solely with uncomfortable pity. In one chapter, 'The Needs of the Dying', she articulates the voice of the dying that she had heard over the years thus: 'I feel so uncertain about my future. Sometimes all I can see in front of me are those future things I am afraid of. And each day my fear ignites a different emotion . . . I want you to see me as a whole person, not as a disease, not as a tragedy.'

She is anxious, too, that people should not imagine there is anything wrong with experiencing great anger over a death: 'Feelings of anger, particularly at a sudden death, are very, very normal to have. These feelings need to be acknowledged and we need to find a responsible way to express them. But anger can stop us in our grieving process if we never go beyond it.'

Christine Longaker now lives in the south of France in a medieval village – '35 people, 300 sheep' – and offers, through the programme in which she works, seminars and training for doctors and nurses. She also campaigns for the introduction of more hospices in North America, Australia and Europe.

Although raised in the Christian faith, she and her husband were agnostic during the time of his dying. After her husband's death she tried to find a teaching that might make some sense of her bereavement and heard the Tibetan Buddhist teacher, Sogyal Rinpoche, in California in 1980. She says she was struck by the practical nature of his advice, and this led her to Buddhism.

'When I went through my bereavement I couldn't imagine a more hellish state, and then I realised I needed a spiritual path so I could find something to support me as well as helping me to deal with future losses.'

The book, despite its rather off-putting, New Agey cover, draws on many religions and much humanist teaching in a way that she hopes will help people 'die well' and their survivors find meaning and a deeper healing from what we all must one day experience.

• *Facing Death and Finding Hope* by Christine Longaker, Arrow, £6.99.

Widows urged to talk about death

By *Christine Newman*

Widows and widowers were urged yesterday to talk about death. On the concluding day of the 8th conference of the International Federation of Widows' and Widowers' Associations (FIAV) in Dublin Castle, the delegates were addressed by Mr Jim Kuykendall, an American bereavement therapist and psychologist based in London.

The federation hopes to work with the EU and a group dealing with bereavement after road accidents.

The general assembly also agreed to hold the next conference in 2001 in Cameroon.

Ms Joan Towle, FIAV president, said speakers during the three-day conference stressed the importance of developing work with the EU.

She said another suggestion had been talks with a group which dealt with bereavement after road accidents. This was an important step as traffic accidents were the third most common cause of death, not only in developed countries but also in countries with fewer cars on the roads.

Ms May Clancy, of the National Association of Widows in Ireland, which organised and hosted the event, closed the session by telling delegates from all over the world that people were coming forward to work on behalf of widows and widowers.

Earlier, Mr Kuykendall, speaking about 'Bereavement as we approach the new millennium', said people were afraid to let go. Most had been brought up in a culture of the stiff upper lip and told to be brave. There were millions of angry women and men who wanted to cry after bereavement but felt it was not acceptable.

Different countries dealt with it differently. In Mediterranean countries, people cried and let their feelings work but did not talk. In Teutonic countries, they talked but did not let their feelings show. 'Ireland seems to have done both. It seems like you've pulled it off somehow,' Mr Kuykendall said.

People should not be ashamed of any thoughts and feelings they might have about a deceased person because of the culture of 'not speaking ill of the dead'. In the new millennium, we should humanise and personalise death and speak clearly and without shame about our losses, he said.

There was a need to break down the conspiracies of silence within families, particularly in not talking about death.

'Maybe in the new millennium we should teach people to continue the dialogue about a person by not always eulogising them and not feeling guilty,' he said.

Attitude to death in Ireland is praised

By Christine Newman

Exploration or analysis of death and the process of bereavement was not morbid but was the very essence of life, Dr Anthony Clare, consultant psychiatrist, told a conference of widows and widowers in Dublin yesterday.

Dr Clare, medical director of St Patrick's Hospital, was addressing more than 200 delegates from around the world on the second day of a three-day conference of the International Federation of Widows' and Widowers' Associations in Dublin Castle.

Speaking on 'Bereavement and Loss in Modern Ireland', Dr Clare said that in Ireland death was accepted and acknowledged. When he returned to Dublin after living in London he saw a funeral at the rush hour on a Friday evening. Traffic came to a halt as the cortege crossed the street. He was struck by the importance the public granted to grieving in the midst of a day's work.

'This may change with the new Celtic Tiger, where, perhaps, such sensitivity may get lost,' he commented.

Irish culture had resisted trends where death was banished to hospitals and institutions and where funerals were bland, hygienic and speedy affairs.

Death ignored may be death deprived, he said.

There were three stages of normal grieving. First, there was lack of reaction, a numbness, a feeling of unreality.

'What helps the process of grieving to be a healing one is the wake, the public funeral. Funeral services enable relations and friends not to mark a death but to celebrate a life,' Dr Clare said.

However, very often a typical Irish funeral could anaesthetise the bereaved; when it was over was when it hit them. People drifted back to their own lives and the gap was felt, and the bereaved felt completely alone.

The second stage was of sleeping badly, weeping often, no zest, intense restlessness, with difficulty concentrating and remembering. There might be feelings of guilt or anger. Some said the physical pain was unbearable, and not for nothing did they speak of heartbreak, Dr Clare said. 'Bereaved people feel embarrassed at losing control and feel social pressure to pull themselves together,' he remarked.

He said this was never more so than at the time of the death of Princess Diana. The British people were accused of hysteria when in fact they wanted to grieve.

There was evidence that a full ventilation of grief was good for a person, and often people had to be encouraged to let go.

The third stage of grieving was that symptoms slowly abated and the bereaved came to terms with what had happened.

'No one who has lost someone close and dear is ever the same again.

We should resist telling them that he or she will get over it and time is a great healer. We never get over death,' Dr Clare said. Death was unfair.

Some people were given a warning and could say all they wanted to say before a loved one died. Others, however, died suddenly after a car accident, heart attack, or stroke.

'One of the messages is that you should tell the living what they mean to you or you may not get the chance. So many people grieve so much because they wished to have said what they didn't,' Dr Clare said.

Some regarded talking about death as morbid, but to see and face death and go on living was to live enriched. 'To pretend it isn't there is a form of pathology.' The conference, hosted by the National Association of Widows in Ireland, continued with workshops on themes including working with the young widow, with people bereaved following traffic accidents, supporting bereaved children, and the mourning process.

Coping with the loss of a loved one

It happens to all of us some time. One day, someone we care for disappears. The loss can make us feel that life is no longer worth living. Here the *Yours* doctor explains how grief can affect us – and how we can find a way through it . . .

Losing someone close to us is the most traumatic event that can happen in our lives. This is particularly important in later life when the loss f a life-long partner does not only mean mourning, but also possible isolation, loneliness and the loss of somebody who was able to offer practical help with everyday problems and chores.

Two in every three women in Britain over the age of 75 are widowed.

Losing a partner, relative or friend is the most common reason for mourning, but there are other causes. Traumatic events such as losing a limb, serious financial loss or the break-up of a marriage can also cause a reaction of grief.

For some the loss of a pet can be particularly upsetting. Older people who have perhaps spent many years in the company of a trusted pet are quite likely to experience strong feelings of grief when their pet dies.

Sometimes these feelings may be even stronger than those experienced after the loss of a human friend.

In this case, sharing the feelings of grief with other people is not only a mark of respect for the lost pet but also a psychological way of helping to recover from grief.

Symptoms

There are certain bodily symptoms associated with grief.

Included are crying spells, diarrhoea, dizziness, sweating, fainting and stomach pains. Apart from the physical problems, there are also psychological problems associated with the reaction of the body to the loss.

Following a loss, whether sudden or expected, we all go through a process of mourning. This is normal and it happens to everybody, although some people are generally less able to cope with sudden change, not only emotionally but also physically. Feeling powerless, lost and confused is common after a sudden change such as the loss of a loved one.

Four stages of recovery

What follows is a description of the four stages of recovery that everyone who has lost a loved one has to go through.

I hope that by knowing what is expected, a person in mourning will find it easier to cope with the loss.

Disbelief

First is the stage if disbelief. This happens immediately after the death and the bereaved person feels anger at the loss, denies that the loss has occurred, and feels emotionally numb.

They might frequently ask themselves, 'Why has this happened to me?' This may last for hours or days.

Despair

After disbelief comes the stage of despair. The bereaved person feels restless, disorganised and may wander around the house looking for their lost partner.

This, in a way, is a wish to confirm that the death has taken place. The bereaved person wants to have another chance to bring the dead person back to life again.

Many people believe that they saw, heard or touched the dead person during the days following the death. This stage may last for days or weeks.

Detachment

The following stage is detachment, when the ties with the dead begin to break, memories of the dead person become less clear and there is a general forgetfulness during everyday life. The loss begins to be accepted but life loses its meaning and its worth.

This is the stage when depression may occur, and although this is normal up to a certain point, it may become more serious, needing medical care.

In most cases this phase lasts for several months.

Acceptance

Finally, there is the stage of adjustment and reorganisation.

The reality of the death is accepted, memories of the dead person become more favourable, there is a return to the previous activities and to everyday routine.

New activities and interests may develop and one may discover a new, more mature self. It is then possible to talk about the death without overwhelming emotional upset.

On average, these stages take about one or two years but the length of each stage varies.

Also, some of these stages may overlap. It is not unusual for an older person to grieve for three or more years, but if any longer, there might be a danger of the whole process becoming too drawn out and difficult to overcome

Apart from these normal stages of grief, some people may feel excessively anxious, and experience severe feelings of guilt and despair. In certain older people, bereavement may become more prolonged than usual and can take years without any improvement.

In others it may be masked. This is called 'inhibited grief' and happens to people who try very hard to hide their emotions from others.

Both of these types of bereavement need to be dealt with by professionals, in order to avoid long-term problems and unnecessary emotional suffering.

Getting support

During bereavement, we all need kindness and support. Kindness should be expected from the friends or relatives of the bereaved and it can be a very strong psychological balm to heal the loss.

Support may also be given by organisations which specialise in helping people who experience a death in their close circle.

Such groups may offer practical help with funeral arrangements, legal issues and other practicalities, as well as psychological help with sympathetic counselling.

Bereavement can take different forms in different cultures. For example, in certain Asian cultures, death is more easily shared by the family and friends, whereas in Western societies death is mainly a reserved, personal affair.

It is easy for the bereaved person to develop depression and this becomes more likely when your emotions are not shared with others.

When a loved one is terminally ill, it is common for feelings of bereavement to start as the loss becomes imminent.

The relatives or friends of a dying person may feel sad, guilty and they may fear being left alone, without realising that this is part of the normal mourning process which began earlier. This can happen days or even weeks before the actual death.

This so-called 'anticipated bereavement', a cold psychological term, is nevertheless very important because it helps both the dying person and the family to prepare for the future.

Whether this helps in reducing the length of the stages of bereavement is not very clear, but it is important to recognise that this may happen and offer help and support to the grieving person. Sudden loss, on the other hand, will not allow for any preparation to happen and it can make the process of bereavement more traumatic.

Once a death has been accepted there should be no further psychological problems and the return to normality should be smooth.

There are, however, certain difficult dates which can cause a relapse of the symptoms of grief – the anniversary of the death, the birth of the dead person, the wedding anniversary, and Christmas or Easter.

Those who offer support to a bereaved relative or friend need to be aware of these dates and they should offer extra help during that time.

It is common for bereaved people to visit their doctor on these anniversaries, complaining of apparently unrelated problems, when what they really need is sympathy and understanding.

Spiritual help becomes more valued even by disbelievers. Bereavement counselling consists of listening, reassuring and offering advice. It is important to allow time for the normal processes of grief to develop and not hurry the process up. Moving house or other serious decisions should be left for a later stage.

Any form of severe stress such as bereavement is associated with an increased risk of illness or even death. This may be related to the weakening of the immune system which fights disease, and is also due to other psychological causes. Paying extra attention to a healthy diet and exercise is important during these difficult times.

Eventually, the recovery from these harsh psychological events will be complete and life will continue with new hope for the future.

Being patient is a virtue which heals most traumatic events in our lives, leaving only warm, happy memories of our loved ones.

© *Yours*
September, 1998

Cruse youth line

How old do I have to be to call?
Old enough to make a telephone call and young enough to be called youth.

Do I have to tell you my name?
No – but you can if you want to. Your counsellor will have a name, too.

Can I call you if my pet dies?
Yes – pets are very important – so are mums and dads and brothers and sisters and grandmothers and granddads and friends and teachers.

Will you tell my parents that I called?
No – we won't tell anyone outside Cruse *unless* we feel you are in any danger – if we have to tell someone we will tell you first.

Will I have to pay for the call?
Yes – I'm afraid this isn't a free line. Do check that it's OK to use the phone and remember – whom you call is recorded on telephone bills and calls from mobile phones can be a lot more expensive than other phones.

Who will answer my call?
A trained bereavement counsellor – that's someone who knows a lot about the feelings and thoughts and problems that affect people when someone dies.

How can you help me?
It all depends on what kind of help you're looking for.
• We can listen to you.
• We can help you understand what makes you feel the way you do.
• We can suggest things to do which might help you.
• We can put you in touch with someone you could go and see.
• We can help you sort out what would be most helpful.

Has someone you know died? Worried? Unhappy? Want help? Why don't you ring the Cruse Youth Line 0181 940 3131 Fri 5-9 pm Sat 11am–6pm. See page 40 for full address details.

© *Cruse*

About bereavement

Information from the London Bereavement Network

Bereavement

Bereavement and loss are things which we all experience at some time in our lives. However, grief expresses itself in many different ways, often with powerful, frightening and confusing feelings. It is common for these feelings to ebb and flow over a very long period of time, whilst those around us may say 'you should be over this by now'. Although no two people's experience will be the same, below are listed some of the common feelings which you may experience at different times in your grief:

Shocked disbelief

You may find yourself being very calm and rather detached. Conversely you may feel completely at sea. Both are perfectly usual reactions.

Being unable to accept the loss

This often involves what has been called searching behaviour, which means that at some level you are trying to deny that the death has occurred, and in so doing you might find yourself making mistakes, which can be worrying. For example thinking that you have seen or heard the dead person, or laying his/her place at the table. You may even find yourself at odd moments of the day actually looking for him or her. Again this is perfectly usual.

Anger and guilt

You may be wanting to ask the questions, Why has this happened? and Why has this happened to me? It is common to wish to find blame for it, either in yourself, in others, or even with the person who has died, and this can lead to powerful feelings of anger and guilt (or sometimes both).

Despair and depression

There may be times when you lose all interest in living and feel that there is no point going on. You may even question your own sanity and think that you are going mad. This, though painful, is a common experience.

Reorganisation

Usually this occurs with the passage of time and, when the pain has eased somewhat, you may find yourself being able to remember without feeling so overwhelmed. This can be a time for you to begin life again, maybe to renew old interests and take up new pursuits. This might seem disloyal to the person who has died, but what has happened in the past is always a part of you and is not affected by your enjoying the present, or planning for the future.

How you can help yourself

As well as going through many of the reactions outlined above, you may also experience many other feelings (e.g. panic, relief, fear, self-pity). If you do experience these emotions you may feel you ought to hide them, but they are an important part of your bereavement and it can be valuable to share them with a sympathetic listener. You may find yourself feeling hurt and convinced that some of your friends are avoiding you. Unfortunately, this often happens and can be due to embarrassment – 'not knowing what to say'. It may be up to you to take the first step to let others know you need them and their support.

It is sometimes very tempting to feel that life would be more bearable if you moved house or quickly disposed of possessions or refused to see people. There is a very common urge to avoid painful things. However, this can make things worse and such decisions must be given great thought. Bereavement is a time of very painful emotions, but it is important to experience these to the full in order to build your life again.

It is not uncommon, as well as feeling mentally taxed, to feel physically run down: to find it difficult to eat, sleep and so on, but eventually these symptoms should fade and disappear. It can also be a very isolating process when you may feel as if no one else could possibly experience what you are going through.

If you feel worried about any of your feelings or would simply like to talk with someone, don't hesitate to approach your GP or your local Bereavement Service.

Many people feel, following a close bereavement, that they would like someone outside their immediate circle of family or close friends, to talk with and confide in. For many different reasons they will turn to one of the numerous Bereavement Counselling and Support organisations that exist across the Greater London area.

The London Bereavement Network (LBN) is the forum to which many of these local services are affiliated. It exists to promote and support good working practices in bereavement care across the capital.

Local services vary from borough to borough. Some are independent voluntary community organisations, others are run by local councils or are attached to hospitals and hospices, whilst others are run by organisations of differing faiths.

Bereavement Services that are affiliated to LBN are committed to offering good quality confidential, free and accessible counselling/support. This work is carried out by trained and supervised volunteers, to support people living or working in their local communities.

© London Bereavement Network (LBN)

Death and dying

Where life surrounds death

Beware the Five Stages of Grief

Few concepts have insinuated themselves into the popular culture as thoroughly as the so-called '5 Stages of Grief': Denial, Anger, Bargaining, Depression, Acceptance. We've heard it from professionals in all areas of the healthcare system (who should know better) as well as from lay persons of all ages (who shouldn't). There is even a lengthy comedy routine about it by Dustin Hoffman playing Lenny Bruce in the movie *Lenny*. The time has now come to ditch it as the concept has done more harm than good.

Three common myths about the 5 Stages

1. The 5 Stages of Grief were defined by Elisabeth Kübler-Ross

In her book *On Death and Dying*, Macmillan Publishing Company, 1969, she presents 5 stages terminally ill persons may go through upon learning of their terminal illness. She presents them as 'an attempt to summarize what we have learned from our dying patients in terms of coping mechanisms at the time of a terminal illness'.

These stages were not originally the 5 Stages of Grief but better: the 5 Stages of Receiving Catastrophic News. Over the next 28 years, healthcare professionals, clergy, nurses, doctors, caregivers, students, and other readers of the book somehow mutated the stages into the 5 Stages of Grief.

2. The 5 Stages define the process a bereaved person must go through in order to resolve their grief.

Grief is a complicated, multi-dimensional, individual process that can never be generalised in 5 steps. In fact, as will be shown, a person will generally have to go through the 5 Stages before true grieving can even begin.

3. A person who isn't progressing through the 5 Stages in sequence and in a timely manner needs professional help.

This common belief has caused a lot of problems and misunderstandings. One researcher has shown that some caregivers have actually gotten angry at the bereaved person for not following the stages in order! The person shouldn't be angry yet because they haven't been through denial.

All of the above points to a basic misunderstanding about what grief is to begin with so it's not surprising that myths continue to propagate. This is most likely because the pervasiveness and impact of grief wasn't really recognized by the psychological community until around the 1980s and even then it was slow in coming.

For example, in 1974 *The Handbook of Psychiatry* defined grief as ' . . . the normal response to the loss of a loved one by death'. Responses to other kinds of losses were labelled 'Pathological depressive reactions'.

In 1984, Dr Terese Rando – a noted grief specialist, researcher and author – defined grief as ' . . . process of psychological, social and somatic reactions to the perception of loss'.

In 1991, the Grief Resource Foundation of Dallas, Texas, found that, for them, a good working and practical definition of grief was 'the total response of the organism to the process of change'.

Today, in December 1996, we at TLC Group have come to accept the Grief Response as the Unified Field Theory of All Mental Illness (a subject of another Tip of the Month!)

Curiously, most non-grief specialists commonly accept the definition of grief given in 1974. So what is grief and what produces it? A helpful equation, which proves itself daily in all instances is: Change = Loss = Grief.

This means that . . .

1. A change of circumstance of any kind (a change from one state to another) produces a loss of some kind (the stage changed from) which will produce a grief reaction.

2. The intensity of the grief reaction is a function of how the change-produced loss is perceived. If the loss is not perceived as significant, the grief reaction will be minimal or barely felt.

3. Significant grief responses which go unresolved can lead to mental, physical, and sociological problems and contribute to family dysfunction across generations.

So, are the 5 Stages without value? Not if they are used as originally intended, as the 5 Stages of Receiving Catastrophic News. One can even extrapolate to the 5 Stages of Coping With Trauma. Death need not be involved.

As an example, apply the 5 Stages to a traumatic event almost all of us have experienced: the dead battery! You're going to be late to work so you rush out to your car, place the key in the ignition and turn it on. You hear nothing but a grind; the battery is dead.

1. *Denial* – What's the first thing you do? You try to start it again! And again. You may check to make sure the radio, heater, lights, etc. are off and then . . . try again.

2. *Anger* – '%$@^##& car!', 'I should have junked you years ago.' Did you slam your hand on the steering wheel? I have. 'I should just leave you out in the rain and let you rust.'

3. *Bargaining* – (realising that you're going to be late for work) . . . 'Oh please car, if you will just start one more time I promise I'll buy you a brand new battery, get a tune up, new tyres, belts and hoses, and keep you in perfect working condition.

4. *Depression* – 'Oh God, what am I going to do. I'm going to be late for work. I give up. My job is at risk and I don't really care any more. What's the use?'

5. *Acceptance* – 'Ok. It's dead. Guess I had better call the Auto Club or find another way to work. Time to get on with my day; I'll deal with this later.'

This is not a trivial example. In fact, we all go through this process numerous times a day. A dead battery, the loss of a parking space, a wrong number, the loss of a pet, a job, a move to another city, an overdrawn bank account, etc. Things to remember are:
1. Any change of circumstance can cause us to go through this process.
2. We don't have to go through the stages in sequence. We can skip a stage or go through two or three simultaneously.

3. We can go through them in different time phases. The dead battery could take maybe 5 to 10 minutes, the loss of a parking space 5 to 10 seconds. A traumatic event which involves the criminal justice system can take years.
4. The intensity and duration of the reaction depends on how significant the change-produced loss is perceived.

It was mentioned above that grieving only begins where the 5 Stages of 'Grief' leave off. Grief professionals often use the concept of 'Grief Work' to help the bereaved through grief resolution. One common definition of Grief Work is summarised by the acronym TEAR:
T = To accept the reality of the loss
E = Experience the pain of the loss
A = Adjust to the new environment without the lost object
R = Reinvest in the new reality

This is Grief Work. It begins when the honeymoon period is over, the friends have stopped calling, everyone thinks you should be over it, the court case is resolved, 'closure' has been effected, and everything is supposed to be back to normal. It's at this point that real grieving begins.

Notice that the first step of Grief Work is acceptance, the last stage of the 5 Stages of Grief. Let's throw out the 5 Stages of Grief and replace it with a greater understanding of Grief Recognition and Resolution.

• The above information is by the TLC Group, Dallas, Texas. Their publications can be obtained via the web site: http://griefnet.org/bookstore.dir/tlc/tlcgroup.html

Studies show that pets can help people cope with bereavement

By Eileen Murphy

The old adage that a dog is man's best friend has been proved by experts studying the effects of a canine companion on widows, drug addicts and the young victims of war.

Researchers from Britain, Italy and Croatia yesterday revealed details of projects looking at the part that pets can play in helping the bereaved, addicted and stressed.

Speaking at an international conference on the changing role of pets in society at Prague in the Czech Republic, June McNicholas, from Warwick University, said dogs offered the highest levels of response to help recently widowed people deal with their emotions.

A study group of 167 widowed people aged between 40 and 75 years was measured.

Another study, conducted by Giampaolo Nicolai in Rome, used a dog-training programme as part of a learning scheme for young drug addicts. The aim was to provide opportunities for the addicts to learn communication and relationship skills.

A conference spokesman said: 'Nicolai found the addicts showed improved self-esteem and motivation from learning to train a dog and through developing closer relationships with pets.'

The third study, carried out in Croatia, looked at three groups of Slavic primary school children to see if those with pets differed in how they coped with the stress and trauma associated with living in a war-torn country.

The results, which will be published soon, showed that children with dogs and cats found it easier to express their emotions and seek social support avoiding the effects of post-traumatic stress disorder.

Pain of loss as a part of life

By John Macleod

A family funeral last week – it was a great-aunt of mine, whom I shall remember for her delicious wit and very private, deeply tested faith – cast my mind on the theme of bereavement. How well do we, these days, cope with shattering personal loss? Nationally, we were confronted with the issue when Diana, Princess of Wales, was killed last September. The tragedy met with a markedly cooler, more sensible reaction this side of the Border. Yet the scenes on television showed the frenzied, posturing hysteria of thousands on the streets of London and elsewhere: scenes of lamentation, ululation more fit for Latin America than to the land of Ealing comedy and *Mrs Miniver's Diary*.

Not all loss, of course, is the black bereavement of death. The end of a passionate love affair has a trauma nearly as raw. Someone undergoing radical surgery – the loss of a limb – is bereaved in another sense.

Then there is the loss of identity and purpose if you are sacked, or made redundant, or forced into unsought retirement by some mandatory age criterion. And, each year of life, we are bereaved in a hundred little ways.

Psychologists speak of the omnipotentiality of youth. The lively teenagers of my acquaintance have all life before them. They face a thousand choices, a thousand options, a thousand turnings, and blaze in mingled hope, exuberance, and apprehension. At 18 or 19 or 20 or even 25 you can still hope to be anything you want to be.

But years go by. The options shrink. Your prospects may yet burn bright; but they inevitably narrow. The path of wisdom is to celebrate the perspective and tenacity we gain with passing decades. Many, however, experience the midlife years as years of crisis: they reach the time when denying the wrinkles, the utterly lost opportunities, goes beyond optimism to psychosis.

Yet there is nothing like the bereavement of death. It is the finality of the thing. The relationship is utterly gone. There is no earthly hope of renewed fellowship. The remains do not begin to resemble the person you knew: they are an empty shell, without spirit, without vitality. She no longer resembles your mother: she looks like the archetypal old woman, both anonymous and universal.

> **The first day or so of close bereavement is shock. It is surprising how coldly and practically one can function**

Perhaps it is all the worse today because we, who as a society have shed all inhibitions about sex and discussion of sexual matters – to the squalid extreme that 10-year-olds tell fellatio jokes – are more and more out of touch with death.

Then at last it strikes close in our family circle, and we see horrors we never knew of before. We had entertained visions of the dear departed whispering his last words surrounded by our decorously weeping selves: we see, instead, days of advancing incoherence, struggle, coma, emaciation, the final organic fight for breath. We had pictured a body palely pink with peaceful smile: we confront a beaky, putty-coloured effigy, looking either gormless or devilish. And so on. We see this, and we think of the hour of our own death, and we think: 'Is that the way it really is: is this my latter end?' Yet still, on the mainland at least, you meet adults who have never attended a funeral: recently I spoke to a man, pushing 50, who had never in his life looked on a dead body.

The first day or so of close bereavement is shock. It is surprising how coldly and practically one can function. Arrangements are made; people are telephoned; things are bought. You cook; you attend to animals; and so on. Then the night comes and you cannot sleep. Sleep,

between death and the funeral, is, for many, quite impossible; and sheer physical, mental exhaustion is a serious part of bereavement.

So the family gather. It is a strange time, for each is drawn into herself or himself and most of the time we are silently brooding and grieving, and yet forced – in the nature of things – to interact, and decide details of beds and wreaths and cars and who sits where; and you are only half-listening, and there are crossed lines and cross-purposes and misunderstandings.

People regress, too, especially if the death is a parent or grandparent.

Self-appointed chief mourners emerge. Tensions creak. Someone wants to be by himself to mourn; someone else insists on a collective family gathering in the parlour. Someone wants to look at photographs; someone else must immerse themselves in physical activity, making mountains of food no one wants to eat.

Someone rabbits on and on in the most garrulous, stream-of-consciousness fashion, until your thoughts verge on the murderous. Most families, I think, in this sore situation, can be sure to throw up a Drama Queen, a Philosopher, a Boss, and a Saint. Sibling rivalries ooze out in the old subtle ways. And yet, too, you find strength where you thought there was only weakness: you see virtues and capacities in loved ones you had never seen before. (When we lost our grandmother, some months ago, I was astonished how much real comfort and strength I could draw from quite small cousins in Stornoway.) But the shock is wearing off and now memories are flooding back – memories upon memories of the departed, things you had never thought you remembered at all. You see something, a photo, or think of something, and tears well up, and then someone asks if you take milk in that tea, and you nearly chew their head off.

In the meantime, of course, you are having visitors. Distant relatives converge, and the atmosphere lightens up a little as old ties are renewed.

Little reconciliations happen. Good men arrive: elders and minis-

ters, gracious ladies with useful things. By now you are conscious of astonishing alertness. Everything has heightened reality. You remember acutely the good and kind things folk say: you also, less happily, remember the stupid and tactless.

And then all is done: the coffin lowered, the cords dropped, the last words said, the soft rain of earth on polished pine. At last the family is alone

---

If I had two rules about expressing condolence, they would be these: say something meaningful to comfort the person you are addressing, and never – whatever – say 'I'm so sorry', which is a phrase both meaningless and presumptuous. It is no sense to ask a lad, 'How's mum?' when he is weeping for his father. And you may be sorry; you may have sad, comfortable thoughts; but you are not sorrowing as she is sorrowing.

The public rites of mourning have their own character: details to be planned, moments of profound feeling, moments of farce. You speculate on those present (and those absent); you wonder, wickedly, 'Is she wearing that hat for a bet?'; you remember who sang off-key; who

stumbled in the lifting of the coffin; who was smelling of whisky, and him a deacon. There is always someone of whom you think, 'Well, he won't have the nerve to turn up', and, sure enough, he does.

You mark cards. A Free Church minister, months ago, entered my all-time hall of ecclesiastical infamy for an orotund, theatrical prayer at the funeral of one who, though a beloved father and a well-liked neighbour, was not Free Church and made no profession of religion. In 14 weary minutes of confident harangue, this cleric consigned a man he scarcely knew to a lost eternity: more, he prayed leaning against the pulpit enclosure, a hand thrust deep in trouser pocket, as hearts broke before him.

And then all is done: the coffin lowered, the cords dropped, the last words said, the soft rain of earth on polished pine. At last the family is alone.

There is a good meal. Suddenly you want to eat, and you dine heartily.

Tension is released: humour bubbles again. You will sleep tonight.

Life is changed, and irrevocably. The loss abides. But the loss becomes part of life, and life becomes newly normal, flowing in good and bad as before, through times of gentle happiness. That is the abiding truth of bereavement.

You never get over it. You just get used to it.

© The Herald
April, 1998

When you lose someone close

On average three out of every 400 schoolchildren lose a close relative each year. In the wake of Princess Diana's death, Peter Kingston asks how schools look after the special needs of bereaved pupils

As a teacher 10 years ago Barbara Ward remembers trying out ideas in the classroom to help youngsters think about bereavement and the bereaved.

'In one fifth form, a girl suddenly started crying,' she recalls. 'Her father had died two years earlier and she said that when she came back nobody in the school mentioned it.'

While working as an advisory teacher in Personal and Social Education in the London borough of Hillingdon, she was putting together two teaching packs on bereavement for schools – one for under-11s, the other for over-11s. But no publishers in the mid-1980s were prepared to produce them, and she had to fund production herself.

'In those days they said that nobody wanted to look at things like that. Now all educational publishers have something on loss and bereavement on their lists.'

But during the Falklands War, she says, schools around the country had become alerted to the knock-on effects on pupils who lost fathers or who were distracted by worries that their fathers would not return from the South Atlantic. Some performed badly in exams. Many could not settle during lessons.

The consensus among specialists in grief counselling is that schools have recently become much better at helping children cope with bereavement.

Many adults who suffered bereavement during their schooldays will recall with bitterness that up to a decade ago things were often very different.

Staff and other pupils were commonly kept in the dark when a child suffered the loss of a parent or other close relative. And as often as not when they were told, adults and children would from embarrassment, or a misplaced sense of compassion, not bring the matter up when the grieving youngster returned to school.

The overwhelming view of counsellors seems now to be that the non-recognition by schools of pupils' losses is one of the gravest errors they can make in the all-too-common occurrence of pupil bereavement.

> *'I think it is appropriate for the form teacher, or a teacher closest to the child, to meet them before they return to school to try to soften the route back'*

They believe all schools need to put together a strategy on responding to bereavement with expert advice, and not find themselves responding on the hoof, because there is a risk that unprepared responses, even though instinctive, may be wrong.

They all agree that there are no neat and simple solutions. Young people are as diverse as adults are in their responses to the death – sudden or anticipated – of someone close. Some want to talk at length, others want to be able to express their grief in other ways, perhaps by drawing, painting or in play, and others don't want to talk at all.

'Children have a right and a need when they are experiencing grief to give it expression,' says Janet Haddington, founder of the National Association of Bereavement Services (NABS), a coordinating organisation which aims to promote the needs of bereaved individuals or families.

She says the key thing is to convey to the child that should he or she wish to talk to someone they trust, whether it be a well-known member of staff or a friend, this opportunity is available. And it is important that the child can feel there are secure conditions at school in which to express feelings.

It is just as important not to crowd grieving youngsters when they return to school, says Carole Lambert, NABS administrator. While staff and schoolmates should acknowledge the death, a continual stream of solicitous enquiries and endless offers of sympathetic ears are likely to be upsetting.

During a bereaved child's absence, the class teacher could discuss the situation with classmates. How might they feel if they were returning to school after a parent's death? What might they need or dread in similar circumstances? What do they think will be their classmate's needs?

'It is good to appeal to the natural compassion of children at times like this,' says Haddington.

At this stage the bereaved's closest friend might be asked if they would be prepared to help, to be a ready sympathetic ear to the child and to be alert to any sudden needs or problems, she says.

'I think it is appropriate for the form teacher, or a teacher closest to the child, to meet them before they return to school to try to soften the route back.'

One reliable generalisation about grieving children is that they want to return to normality as soon as possible, says Carole Lambert, NABS administrator. 'In their school life at least, things are back to normal, their routine carries on, their friends are there. Because at home everything is out of control and out of order.'

Children often seem to bounce back from bereavement more quickly than adults do. If, days after the awful event, a child is laughing and playing with schoolfriends, he or she should not be made to feel this is in any way wrong, the specialists agree.

'Children can't remain sad for too long,' says Janet Haddington. 'But as with adult mourners they are likely to experience a trigger which reawakens the pain and all they are feeling.'

Schools should be prepared for oscillating mood swings from mourning pupils for long periods after the loss. The anger that people can feel after a loved one's loss is often magnified in children, for whom death has not become a familiar experience. And the loss of a parent is a shattering blow to a child's sense of security. These strong emotions are commonly released against the school and children who were previously well-behaved become disruptive and rebellious.

Grief intensifies the problems of adolescence, a traditionally difficult time, says Carole Lambert. The insecurities of this half-child/half-adult stage are magnified.

A particularly dangerous time comes when the surviving parent meets a new partner or makes a new friend of the opposite sex. All this can trigger attention-seeking behaviour, including excessive abuse of alcohol, tobacco and other drugs, and sexual promiscuity, says Lambert.

'Schools should at the very least be aware of these possibilities and be prepared to make allowances.'

Pretending nothing has happened is the worst thing you can do for grieving children, away from their families. The Bloxham Project is a scheme designed to teach teachers how to cope

Few grimmer tasks face boarding schools than coping with youngsters mourning the death of a parent. Horrible as it is to break the news of a parent's or sibling's sudden death to a young person during term-time, it can be even trickier to receive a mourning youngster back after a vacation bereavement, according to Rev. Gregory Cameron, a former school chaplain with long experience of helping bereaved young boarders.

'This is because you are not part of the beginning of the process but coming into it halfway,' he says. 'There is a real danger of pretending nothing has happened and trying to carry on as normal.'

At least Princes William and Harry, as they go back for the start of the autumn term, are likely to find a more enlightened reception than in earlier times. Finding strategies for approaching bereavement is on the agenda of most independent schools now, says Cameron, who runs the Bloxham Project, a scheme providing training and advice to independent schools with spiritual and pastoral concerns.

For one thing, the staff profile in boarding schools differs radically from that of the late 60s when the project was launched. 'Thirty years ago, the typical independent school common room was made up of bachelors who had been through the same system,' says Cameron.

Most children, like most adults, prefer their loss to be acknowledged by those they live and work with, but not to be forced into long conversations about it

---

'Now the staffs are much more heterogeneous. The majority of these common rooms are filled with people who have been through the state system.'

The change in the breed of boarding-school teacher or carer might mean the stiff-upper-lip approach is a thing of the past. But it does not guarantee good approaches to bereavement. Staff need to be helped to prepare for it, says Cameron.

A prime aim of the Bloxham training courses is to help staff understand what it is to go through a bereavement. The emotions released during these sessions have been an eye-opener, Cameron says. 'You might have three or four teachers in tears. You find yourself putting teachers in touch with their own bereavements which very often they might not have worked through.'

Another aim is to help teachers realise that with bereavement, they are not there to provide solutions. 'The role of the teacher changes from someone who has an answer to someone who will be a companion to a bereaved child and will walk with the child through the experience.'

In the training sessions, teachers are urged to respect children's feelings. There should be no 'pull yourself together' or 'If I were in your position I would…' approaches.

Children in mourning will often have concerns which appear trivial to adults, says Cameron. 'Mum's died. Who's going to take me swimming?' should not be dismissed. William and Harry will probably be thinking: 'We used to have so much fun with mum – who'll do that for us now?'

Such concerns do not mean the grief is superficial, he says. 'Grief hits children in a different way that needs to be respected.'

Most children, like most adults, prefer their loss to be acknowledged by those they live and work with, but not to be forced into long conversations about it. The key need is the freedom to talk, or not to talk, about the bereavement.

It is essential that other pupils have been informed by the school, says Cameron. And some who are closest to the bereaved can be encouraged to be part of the support network he or she needs. 'I think there is scope for senior pupils to be given rudimentary training in counselling so they can help.'

Independent schools, like their maintained counterparts, are becoming more aware of the fall-out of bereavement – the rage some young people feel, the bad behaviour, the attention-seeking, and sometimes the desire to drop out. They have become more flexible about these after-effects and the need to give the youngsters space, says Cameron. He reckons it is more helpful to talk through grief rather than bottle it up, but at a time and place of the bereaved's choosing.

How long grief lasts is impossible to measure, he says. 'It can take three months or 20 years.'

© *The Guardian*
September, 1997

17

Grief and the adolescent

By Linda Cunningham

nfortunately, the needs of the bereaved teenager have been sorely overlooked for decades. In many grief recovery programmes, support is often available for younger children and adults, but there is a definite void in teen services. I have seen this void throughout our country.

Teenagers often give us mixed messages. They tell us that they need and expect our help in providing them with food and a nurturing environment but also tell us, on the other hand, that they can run their lives on their own. Because people do not always know how to respond to teens, they frequently back off, resulting in a teen who is left to grieve alone or with very limited support.

What makes adolescent grief different from that experienced by an adult?

Adolescence is perhaps one of the most difficult and confusing stages in life. It is a time of change and with every change comes a grieving process. As an example:

- The teenager who has a brother or sister move out of the house to get married or go to school will have to adjust to life in the home without their sibling. Meals and family events will not be spent together with the frequency of the past.
- Divorce in a family will also bring about a grieving process as one parent leaves the home.
- Children who have been abused or sexually molested will experience the loss of innocence and control of their bodies – a very painful grieving process.
- The dating process, a very natural process in adolescence, also involves grief as relationships build and then dissolve as they discover who they are and what they want in life.

- Death of a pet. A pet is one of the few sources of unconditional love that life affords us. We can tell a pet our secrets, and in most cases, the pet is always glad to see us. Losing a pet can bring about profound grief in many children and adults alike.
- Abortion. Whether we are in agreement or disagreement with the issues of abortion, when it occurs, there is a very real loss that is experienced by both the mother and father. This loss frequently comes back to the surface as other pregnancies occur later on in life.

These are only a few of the grief issues that a teen may experience as a natural part of growing up. Add to these experiences the death of a loved one, and you are likely to find a child who is terribly confused and in great pain.

Experiences of the bereaved teenager

Because grief can be very complex and unique to every individual, we

will address the more frequent reactions of teenagers who are grieving.

Shock/disbelief

Knowing, intellectually, that someone has died does not always mean that the death seems real, especially in the early days and weeks of bereavement. Many teens experience what I call 'automatic pilot': they function as usual but with a feeling that 'this really didn't happen'. Teenagers, in particular, may show little signs of grieving in the beginning. This numbness or form of denial is an important coping mechanism and should be respected. In months to come, the numbness will fade and they will need you more than ever. If the teenager witnesses a traumatic death, this state of shock and disbelief could last for months. Be prepared for signs of post-traumatic stress such as flashbacks, nightmares, etc.

Guilt

Most people who grieve experience some level of guilt. We put ourselves through the If onlys: If only I could have prevented the death; If only I hadn't had that argument; If only I had said 'I love you.' Arguments are a part of family life, especially during adolescence. Because of this fact, teenagers often experience extreme feelings of guilt or take on responsibility for the death in some way. It is important that we do not try to 'fix' their grief. Most teens simply need to tell you what they are feeling and, in time, the guilt, with good support, can diminish.

Unusual happenings

It is not at all uncommon for a bereaved teenager to hear the voice of the deceased or feel as though they see that person passing by or in a crowd. These occurrences can be frightening unless there is someone around to let them know that this is a natural part of the grieving process.

Thoughts of suicide

It is not uncommon for a teenager to have thoughts of suicide as a way of escaping pain or joining their loved one. It is important that these thoughts can be shared in a safe environment without the fear of judgment or panic from the person who is listening. Wanting to escape the pain is a normal response. When teens are made aware of the fact that these thoughts often accompany grief, that in itself can offer some relief.

This subject should always be handled with great care. If the teenager is describing to you a method of how they plan to take their life, this is clearly a 'red flag' and professional help should be made available immediately.

Sexual activity

It is not unusual for a teenager to become sexually active during the grief process. If the teen has lost a family member, frequently other family members will not be available for them emotionally, because they, too, are in pain. The need to be close to someone, both physically and emotionally, can be very strong at this time and sexual activity can also serve as a distraction from their pain.

Drugs/alcohol

When teens are grieving, it is a very natural response to want to numb the pain – when someone is drunk or high, they do not have to feel.

Bereaved teens are at high risk of involving themselves in self-destructive behaviour. While these drugs may temporarily numb the pain, they very clearly prolong and complicate the grieving process. It is important to be open with the teenager in this area without pointing a judgmental finger.

Anger

When we have been abandoned through death, anger can become very powerful. Many teens have said 'I want to punch someone out' or 'I want to destroy something.' It is important that teens be given healthy options in expressing their anger. Some suggestions might include: screaming into a pillow; pounding a mattress; ripping Kleenex out of a box until it is empty; throwing ice cubes at a wall or nearby tree. All of these expressions of anger release the physical energy that words alone cannot. It is important to note, also, that none of these expressions of anger will hurt the teenager or those around him or her.

Tears

Tears are a natural and necessary part of grief. If you do not see the tears, do not assume they are not there. Many teens will grieve privately, crying in the shower, in their rooms or alone at the gravesite. If a teenager should share their tears with you, be still, be quiet and listen – don't try to fix their pain.

How can you help?

Every teenager needs to grieve in their own time and in their own way.

To try and speed up the recovery process could be harmful. Listed below are some suggestions for helping the bereaved teenager.

- Ask to see a picture of the person who has died. Let them tell you about this person and why they were special. Have them share some special memories with you.
- Let the teenager tell you about their experience with the death; where they were when the death occurred, what happened immediately afterwards and what they are experiencing right now. Adults who avoid the subject or put on a front may create an atmosphere of isolation and confusion.

The teenager may assume others really didn't love the deceased. They may also assume, because others do not appear to be grieving, that there must be something wrong with them – this can be very frightening.

- Let the teen tell you about any dreams they have had regarding the death of their loved one. Dreams can be very powerful and a listening ear can provide needed support.
- Writing a letter to the deceased can often provide an opportunity for the teenager to say goodbye to their loved one. While this can be a painful exercise, it frequently provides relief and a safe expression of feelings. Writing a letter to someone they love who is still alive can also be helpful. Many times teens will distance themselves from loved ones fearing that they could lose again and it would be more pain than they could bear. This letter can help them to reconnect with the important people in their lives.
- Making a collage can be a creative way of enhancing the healing process in grief. Let the teenager gather magazines and cut out words and pictures that remind them of the deceased and place them on construction paper. When they complete this project, they will find that they have told a story through their collage. These collages become treasured items. Frequently they are placed in a visible place in the home where people visiting will ask questions about them, affording the teen the opportunity to talk about their loved one without having to bring up the subject themselves.
- Help the teenager identify what they need during this time and encourage them to let others know what they need. The common complaint of many bereaved is that people don't seem to care and they are not around when you need them. Frequently people are not around because they don't know what to do or say and they back off for fear of creating more pain. If we don't tell people what we need, we remain a victim and victims seldom heal.

Remember, even though the teenager is striving for independence, he or she still needs you! Your presence and the expression of genuine support will be a gift they can carry with them for a lifetime.

© TAG: Teen Age Grief, Inc., California, USA

Death in the family

Helping children cope

How does a child respond to death?

When a family member dies, everyone in the family is affected. Children react very differently from adults. Their response will depend upon a number of factors.

Relationship

What type of relationship the person who has died had with the child and the family will affect the response. Loss of a parent, brother or sister will have a very different impact from the loss of a more distant relative. The impact on the child will depend a lot on how closely involved the dead person was in the daily life of the child and family.

Age and level of understanding

The child's level of understanding and how the death affects life in practical terms are major factors. Infants may feel the impact of loss mainly in the way it affects the way in which they are handled, and their daily routine. They are very sensitive to the unhappy feelings of those around them, and may become anxious, difficult to settle and needy of attention. Pre-school children usually see death as temporary and reversible – a belief reinforced by cartoon characters who 'die' and 'come to life' again.

Children between the ages of five and nine begin to think more like adults about death. They are able to understand basic facts, for example that death happens to all living things, has a cause, and involves permanent separation. They can also understand that dead people do not need to eat, drink, do not see, hear, speak or feel. Teenagers are able to understand death in much more adult terms, and to be aware of the feelings of others.

Young children often do not appear sad. They may show their sadness briefly, and at unexpected moments. This may mislead adults into thinking that they have not been affected by the death. Children tend to express their feelings through behaviour rather than words. Most children show anger and anxiety as well as sadness about death. Anger is a natural reaction to the loss of someone who was essential to the child's sense of stability and safety. Anger may be shown in boisterous play, nightmares, or irritability. Often, the child will show anger to surviving family members. Anxiety is shown in 'babyish' talk and behaviour, and demanding food, comfort and cuddles. Younger children believe that they cause what happens around them. They may fear that they caused the death by being naughty. Teenagers may find it difficult to put their feelings into words, and may not show their feelings openly, for fear of upsetting others.

Circumstances of the death

The circumstances of the death affect the impact on the child. Each family responds in its own way to death. Religion and culture will have an important influence on what happens. Other factors that can make a big difference from the child's point of view are:

- How traumatic the death was. A traumatic death is harder to cope with.
- Whether the death was sudden or expected, a relief from suffering or a crushing blow.
- The effect of grief on other family members may mean that they are not able to cope with giving the child the care that is needed.
- How much practical support is available to help the family cope.

Helping a child to cope with death

Being aware of how children normally respond to death makes it easier for an adult to help. It also makes it easier to identify danger signals.

Early stages

Adults sometimes try to shield children from what has happened by withholding information from them. However, experience shows that children benefit from knowing what has happened as soon as possible, and may want to see the dead relative. The closer the relationship, the more important this is. Adults can also help children to cope by listening to the child's experience of the death,

answering their questions, and reassuring them. Children often fear abandonment by loved ones, or fear that they are to blame for the death. Being able to talk about this, and express themselves through play, helps them to cope and also prevents emotional disturbances later in life.

Young children often find it difficult to recall memories of a dead person without being reminded of them. This lack of memory can be very distressing for them. A photograph can be a great source of comfort. Children usually find it helpful to be included in family activities such as attending the funeral. Thought may need to be given as to the support and preparation a child will need in order to be able to do this. A child who is frightened about attending a funeral should not be forced to go. However, (except for very young children) it is usually important to find a way to enable them to say goodbye. For example, lighting a candle, saying a prayer or visiting the grave.

Later on

Once children accept the death, they are likely to display their feelings of sadness, anger and anxiety on and off over a period of time, and often at unexpected moments. The surviving relatives should spend as much time as possible with the child, making it clear that the child has permission to show his or her feelings openly or freely. Sometimes a child may 'forget' that the family member has died, or persist in the belief that he or she is still alive. This is normal in the first few weeks following a death, but may cause problems if it continues.

Warning signs and danger signals

- An extended period of depression, with loss of interest in daily activities and events.
- Inability to sleep, loss of appetite, prolonged fear of being alone.
- Acting like a much younger child for an extended period.
- Denying that the family member has died.
- Imitating the dead person excessively.
- Repeated statements about wanting to join the dead person.
- Withdrawal from friends.
- Sharp drop in school performance or refusal to attend school.

These warning signs indicate that professional help may be needed. A child and adolescent psychiatrist or child psychotherapist can help the child to accept the death and also assist the survivors to find ways of helping the child through the mourning process. Your GP will be able to offer you help and advice, and can refer you and your child to your local Child and Adolescent Mental Health Service where the team includes child psychiatrists, psychologists, social workers, psychotherapists, and specialist nurses.

Source of further information

Heegard, M. (1991) *When Someone Very Special Dies: Children can Learn to Cope with Grief*. Minneapolis: Woodland Press.

Death story wins child book prize

By Dan Glaister,
Arts Correspondent

Last year it was drugs. This year one of the leading children's book prizes has gone to a novel dealing with death and bereavement, but its author denies that its success is connected to the mourning over the death of Diana, Princess of Wales.

River Boy by Tim Bowler was yesterday awarded the prestigious Carnegie Medal. Last year's prize was won by *Junk*, a story of heroin addiction by Melvyn Burgess.

Mr Bowler was inspired to write the book, which tells the story of a girl coming to terms with her grandfather dying, by the death of his own grandfather when he was 14. 'I wanted to write a book about death and dying that would not be preachy or morbid,' Mr Bowler said yesterday. 'It is something that will have resonance for many people because the death of a grandparent is the first experience they will have of dying.' Mr Bowler agreed that the book, which is aimed at a 12-plus age range, was timely. 'I wouldn't say that it was timely in the sense that Diana died or the death of the three children in Drumcree, but it is timely in that it is something that is always with us. To shy away from a theme like this just because it is written for children is absolute nonsense.'

Tricia King, chairman of the panel which selects the winner, said: 'This book is an antidote to the Cool Britannia culture of slick, superficial emotions. *River Boy* deals with one of life's profoundest challenges – coping with the loss of someone you love. Thank God the next generation can draw on imaginative literature of this calibre in helping make sense of life – and death.' *River Boy* is Mr Bowler's third novel. After leaving the University of East Anglia, where he studied Swedish, he worked in a variety of jobs.

His first novel, *Midget*, took 10 years to write, and was published in 1994 when he was 41. His fourth novel, *Shadows*, will be published in January.

He receives the Carnegie Medal, awarded by the Library Association, and £1,000 worth of books, which he plans to donate to his local library in Totnes, Devon.

Previous winners of the Carnegie Medal include C.S. Lewis, Mary Norton and Arthur Ransome.

Bereavement

Information from ChildLine

Many more people now live to an older age than at any time in history. This is mainly due to advances in medicine and social conditions that have occurred in recent years. As a result, far fewer children experience the death of a 'loved one' (a parent, other relative or friend).

The loss or death of someone they care for is likely to be deeply distressing for a child. Loss can come about as the result of an illness, such as cancer; an accident, such as a car crash; or old age. Children can also face the loss of a loved animal or pet. This can be as significant as losing a relative or friend.

Bereavement is the word used to describe the loss that people feel when someone close to them dies.

Grief is the emotion that people go through as a result of the loss of someone they loved.

The way people react to death depends on:
- the age of the bereaved person (young children do not have as clear an understanding as older children); and
- their relationship with the person who has died.

Some common reactions to bereavement

Each individual's reaction will be different and it is impossible to predict how someone will respond.

There are, however, certain reactions that are common to children as well as adults.

- Denial – Some people find it difficult to accept that the person has died. This can take a number of forms, including constantly talking about him or her as if they were still alive.
- Guilt – Some people feel guilty, perhaps for still being alive or for feeling in some way responsible for the death.
- Anger – Some people feel angry towards the dead person for dying; at others who were close to that person, such as a surviving parent; or at others who have not suffered a loss.
- Fear – Some people may have a fear of death, either their own or that of someone else close to them. This fear can often lead to strong attachments being formed to a close friend or surviving parent. It can also lead to practical fears such as who is going to look after them.
- Physical complaints – These include loss or increase in appetite, nightmares, feeling tired, stomach aches or headaches.

Understanding the concept of death depends on the age of the child

- Very young children (under 5 years) tend to think of death as something that is temporary and that the person (or pet) who has died will eventually return. Their response may include feelings of being left behind, fear and insecurity.
- Slightly older children (around 5-8 years) have a greater understanding of death, recognising that it is irreversible. However they can find it difficult to understand their emotional reaction to it, such as feelings of guilt or fear.
- Children aged around 8 years and older have a more realistic understanding about death and the implications of permanent separation. They tend to react with similar emotions to an adult, such as extreme sadness and anger.

In situations other than death, people experience similar emotions to those described above, for example the loss of something that holds a great deal of emotional value for that person, such as splitting up with a good friend or a girl or boyfriend after an argument.

Sometimes people experience the same events with different feelings and emotions. For example, one child moving to another part of the country may be positive and excited, but another may view this with fear and experience grief for the friends, family and familiar environment left behind.

What children have told ChildLine

ChildLine received 840 calls and letters from children about bereavement in the year 1995-1996.

Children and young people call at various stages after a death; some in the immediate aftermath, some many years later. Some calls describe the reactions of other people and how they find it difficult to know how to respond to a person who has been bereaved.

- Laura, 10, described the hurt she feels when she thinks about the death of her little brother, 'my body gets tight, it's as if it's being squeezed together'.

- Simon, 16, contacted ChildLine as he had just been told that his father was dying of cancer and did not have long to live. 'I can't talk to anyone about this, I'm scared of crying in front of them.'
- Veronica's grandmother died in a car crash a year before. She described the feelings she gets when she spends a night at her friend's house. 'I want to have fun, but I feel scared that something will happen to my mum.'
- Mark, who was 14, called to say that his friend had died a few days earlier. He told the ChildLine counsellor that he felt sad and low. 'I didn't even get a chance to say goodbye.'

How ChildLine can help

It is often difficult for children to talk to others about their feelings. For example, a child may feel concerned about upsetting a surviving parent further, or that the surviving parent would be too sad to listen.

ChildLine offers a chance for children and young people to talk about their feelings and emotions in confidence. ChildLine can be contacted free, 24 hours a day, on 0800 1111, or write to ChildLine, Freepost 1111, London N1 0BR.

A Minicom service is also available free on 0800 400222 (2pm to 9pm daily).

© ChildLine

Student counselling

Bereavement

Introduction

Different culture groups have different ways of marking the death of someone they love. Some mourn in a way which celebrates the life of the deceased; others make a great and visible show of their grief. Traditionally, we in Britain are generally very low key in our response to death, marking it with a funeral and perhaps a gathering afterwards, but with no recognised period of mourning and often no great show of feeling. This can leave people feeling very alone in dealing with the intense personal emotions they may be experiencing.

Your own grief

The death of someone who is significant to you is one of the hardest things you will experience in your life. Whether it is expected or a shock, the enormity of loss is something that impacts on you in a very profound way.

Grief takes a long time to work through. There are no hard and fast guidelines for this. It takes as long as it takes, but as a general rule it will take longer than you expect. It is important not to try to 'get over it' too quickly, not to adopt a 'stiff upper lip' attitude. Grief is an inevitable and human response. If suppressed,

it may well surface at some later, less appropriate stage. Sometimes there seems to be an expectation that you will have recovered after a certain time has elapsed, but everyone has their own recovery time which cannot be hurried. The first anniversary of the death is an important milestone and can be particularly difficult. Subsequent birthdays and anniversaries can be poignant reminders of your loss, and you may need to find your own way of dealing with such times by either marking them as special commemorative events or by ensuring you distract yourself while time passes.

Bereavement is an entirely individual experience. No one can tell you how you will or should feel. Everyone grieves in their own special way but there are some generally accepted and recognised reactions:
- You may at first feel totally numb, as if paralysed

Whether it is expected or a shock, the enormity of loss is something that impacts on you in a very profound way

---

- You may find yourself unable to believe the person really is dead
- You may find yourself very angry at being deserted
- You may feel an enormous sense of unfairness
- You may find yourself crying uncontrollably and unable to function as normal
- You may feel guilty about surviving, about not having said goodbye; about leaving things unresolved
- You may feel an aching void, as if you have lost a limb, which you feel will never be filled again
- You may be traumatised if the death has been in any way violent such as through an accident, suicide or murder.

The reaction of others

You will be aware that people around you will react in very different ways to your grief.

There will be those who very much want to help in practical ways, or by giving you emotional support. It is up to you to guide them as to how they may best help you; whether you need a listening ear, or maybe need to be left alone for a while. Remember, they can't know what will help unless you tell them. Don't be afraid to take up offers of help; it is not a sign of weakness to lean on someone when you need support.

There will be others who are unable to cope with your grief, who may not be able to talk about the death or even acknowledge it. This is usually either because it raises profoundly difficult feelings in them, or because they simply don't know what to do or say. This can seem very hurtful if you don't understand what may be behind this seemingly unfeeling behaviour, but it is not uncommon.

How can you help yourself?

Here are some suggestions which you may find helpful:

- Recognise that mourning takes its time and you cannot hurry it along.
- Allow yourself to cry, scream or shout and forgive yourself for doing so at 'inappropriate' moments if that is what you need to do. Don't feel guilty about doing so, even if you feel others are critical of you.
- Accept whatever help you are offered from friends, relatives, religious ministers etc.
- Recognise your need to talk about the deceased, even if you need to do so over and over again, and allow yourself to do so until the need lessens.
- If you are worried about over-using friends, talk to a Student Counsellor or other professional helper.
- If and when you feel ready, consider reading some of the literature on death and loss. Some books are suggested below. You may find this useful and comforting.
- Think about concrete ways of doing something to ease your pain. Would it help to write a letter to the deceased saying what you perhaps didn't manage to say in their lifetime? Would you like to plant a tree or shrub in their memory and watch it blossom? Could you light a candle in remembrance on special days?
- Do whatever you need to do, recognising that this is a most testing and difficult times in your life.

And afterwards . . .

The pain gradually lessens. It does happen even though you think it never will. But with that might come guilt and worry about forgetting or letting go of the dead person. At this stage it may become quite hard to let go of the grief because that is what links you to the deceased. It is important to allow yourself to let go. Along the years, although the pain lessens, the memories will never leave you as the death finds its place in your history and experience. The more easily you can accept the need to grieve, the more comfortably it will rest.

Books

The Courage to Grieve, Judy Tatelbaum. A very understanding book about many aspects of grief and mourning

Facing Grief: Bereavement and the Young Adult, Susan Wallbank. Specifically written for age 18-28 and dealing with specific losses e.g. grandparent, sibling, partner, baby, friend.

A Special Scar: The Experience of People Bereaved by Suicide, Alison Wertheimer. Well constructed, helpful and compassionate.

All these books are recommended by CRUSE.

Coping with pet loss

Information from the British Small Animal Veterinary Association (BSAVA)

Pets are considered an integral part of family life for more than 11.5 million households in the UK. It is not surprising, therefore, that people often mourn a pet's death and experience feelings of grief.

To help owners come to terms with pet loss, Petsavers has published a leaflet called *Coping with the Loss of your Pet*. The leaflet has been written with advice from a pet bereavement counsellor and aims to help reassure people that their reaction to losing their pet is a normal response. It is hoped that the leaflet, which is available for distribution through veterinary practices, will also prove helpful to practice staff counselling recently bereaved owners.

For children, the loss of a family pet may be their first encounter with death. The leaflet therefore provides useful advice on helping children to say goodbye to their dead pet and let go of their grief. If the family later decides to introduce a new animal into the household, they can then do so without feeling that they have deserted their previous pet.

Many adults need a sympathetic ear to help them cope with their bereavement, especially if the circumstances of the loss are distressing, or when there is no one among their friends and relatives who understands their sense of loss. Petsavers has therefore included details of the Society for Companion Animal Studies' Befriender Service helpline. This comprises a network of trained volunteers or 'befrienders' who provide the support and comfort that bereaved pet owners often need.

- Members of the BSAVA can receive copies of the Petsavers leaflet *Coping with the Loss of your Pet* free of charge for distribution to their clients. Further information from BSAVA Cheltenham.

How do you live with the death of a child?

After the death of a child, how best can bereaved parents move on with their lives? By Virginia Ironside

want to make sure something is done so that children are properly screened in the future.' Grahame Livingstone, father of 21-month-old Michael, who died of undetected heart failure on Sunday, has one way of coping with his little boy's death: he needs to make sure that it will not happen again.

Why? What happened? Could I have prevented it? Who is to blame? These are some of the questions that people ask when they are bereaved, and often they cannot rest until they find the answers.

Ten years after Julie Ward's death, a Kenyan gamekeeper has been charged with her murder. Her father, John, can finally say: 'Now, at last, I can get on with my life.' But why did he need this? After all, his daughter will never come back. What has been the point of spending the 10 years, a quarter of a million pounds and 80 trips to Kenya to discover her murderer?

Julie's mother explains: 'I desperately want to know what happened and why. It is only when you know these answers that you can understand and accept it. This is not about punishment. It is about finding out why this happened.'

Answering the question 'why' is the reason that Caroline Dickinson's father will never rest until he has tracked down the murderer of his daughter, in France. 'I have got to move forward,' he says. 'My main priority is that the murderer is found, and to ensure that safety in hostels is improved.'

The parents of Stephen Lawrence have moved heaven and earth to find answers. They did not get any at the recent public inquiry but they found some relief from seeing the faces of the people they believe murdered their son, and hearing the witnesses to Stephen's death.

Knowledge is comforting since however bad it is, however gruesome, nothing can be worse than what your imagination can produce if you let it ramble. Knowledge about what happened helps to lay a person to rest. Knowledge usually brings home the fact that the death was inevitable; there was nothing anyone could have done to prevent it happening. Knowledge of what occurred is a victory over feelings of guilt – an emotion that nearly always features strongly after the death of a loved one.

Then there is anger. Parents of children who die in hospital sometimes rage against doctors, who have often given their very best service to save them. Or they rail against tiny things, such as the nurse forgetting to put sugar in their tea. They need someone on whom to focus their anger. Discovering who killed their loved ones is a way of getting revenge. Ernest Peters, whose wife Wendy died of peritonitis after her bowel was pierced during an operation, was offered £195,000 in compensation. But compensation wasn't what his distress was about. 'When she died, I wanted to pin someone to the wall,' Mr Peters has said. 'Solicitors do not think in those terms. For them, it just boils down to the settlement figure. They weren't interested in investigating the causes. Everyone needs to have a look at what is going on so that it doesn't happen again. I want someone hauled over the coals.'

> *Finding out what happened can often result in steps being taken to ensure that it does not happen again*

John and May MacGalliard got £50,000 when their daughter Lorraine died from septic shock after a series of blunders by doctors who failed to realise that she had an ovarian cyst. 'This was not about money,' they said. 'Those doctors ignored a girl in pain. We wanted to go to court to get the truth.' And Margaret Connor, whose daughter Janine died during an operation to have her ears pinned back, said: 'They've offered us a settlement, but we don't want it. We want our day in court. We just want answers.'

Finding out what happened can often result in steps being taken to ensure that it does not happen again. In this way, the parents can feel that their child didn't die in vain – that the child's short life did achieve something, even though he or she did not live long enough to achieve anything in adulthood.

Anthony Misiolek lost his daughter in the M40 minibus crash; she died partly because there were no seat-belts fitted in the minibus. He has devoted much time to trying to tighten up the laws on seat-belts. Suzy Lamplugh's mother Diana set up a trust in her daughter's name to help protect women against predatory strangers, and Colin Parry, whose son Tim was killed in an IRA bomb blast, has since lectured on peace in Northern Ireland.

Getting to the bottom of things is also a way of continuing to look after a child, even after he or she is dead. When your child is bullied at school, you speak to the head teacher, or confront the bully in the playground. If you did nothing, you would be failing your child. Finding out who killed your son or daughter and bringing them to justice is the final, saddest, act of parenting.

© *The Independent*
August, 1998

Common myths about the death of your child

'Great spirits have always encountered violent opposition from mediocre minds.' – Albert Einstein

Myth: The younger the child/baby, the less intense your pain should be.

Truth: It may be true that society grants us less of a right to grieve for infants and stillborn babies; however, the truth is that the love of a parent is not contingent upon the amount of time we had with our child. Love simply cannot be measured in time. Some may try to 'prorate' our grief. That is, if a ten-year-old dies, it is worth 'x' amount of pain. . . if a one-year-old dies, it is worth 'y' amount of pain . . . if a one-day-old dies, that is worth only 'z' amount of pain. It seems ridiculous to bereaved parents, doesn't it?

Consider this . . . Would it be easier to bury your child when you did or would it be easier to bury them one year later? It is an impossible question to answer. There is no easier time, no lesser pain. It is horrible whenever it happens.

Myth: It has been six months, you should be over this by now.

Truth: The truth is, you will never 'be over' this pain. The pain never completely leaves. We will grieve our entire lifetime for the child we should have with us. When others think we should have gotten over it by now, they are confusing the significance of the death of a child with an event of much lesser significance.

You get over the loss of a job, a broken bone or a friendship gone awry. The death of a child, at any age and from any circumstance, is a life-changing and tragic event that will never be forgotten. You will, however, eventually learn the skills necessary to assist you in dealing with the pain. Day-to-day life will never be 'normal' and may never feel the way it used to, but time does help to ease the pain.

Myth: Sleeping pills, anti-depressants or alcohol will help to get you through this pain.

Truth: Some parents who take pills or use alcohol after the death of their child; eventually realise that they may have been postponing the inevitable. Grief is hard work. Physically exhausting and mentally draining, it is. But I compare grief to a loan. We must all pay back the loan to the rightful owner . . . eventually. The longer we wait to pay the money back, the higher the interest rates and penalties. Accept and embrace the depth of the grief as a normal reaction to the most difficult experience a human could endure.

Myth: Another baby is the answer to the grief.

Truth: Your deceased child's life is worthy of all the pain you feel. While another child will fill your empty, aching arms, it will never replace your other child. Allow yourself time to grieve your child. Do not rush yourself. Another baby may add more pressure on you, your surviving children, your spouse and your new child. Be cautious not to venture into an unprepared pregnancy too soon after the death of your beloved child.

Myth: You need to forget your child and go on with your life.

Truth: Many people will ridicule you if photographs of your deceased child are placed in your home, if you still attend support group meetings or if you memorialise your child years after his or her death. Your faithfulness to your child's memory is to be commended! Do not let others discourage your gift of dedication. The truth is, twenty years after the death of Elvis Presley, the whole country stops to recognise him with candlelight vigils in Graceland. The event is televised world-wide on CNN and every other news station and television station in the country. This is a completely acceptable practice which millions of Americans, young and old, partake in. Yet, the same communities would have grieving parents questioning their own sanity when they chose to participate in an event quietly memorialising someone far more important in their life – their own child. Remember your child. Do not let others determine what is right for you. Remember and do not be ashamed!

Myth: You will soon become yourself again.

Truth: The truth is, you probably died with your child. You may have remnant pieces of the former self remaining; however, you are unlikely to become exactly who you were before. Get to know who you are once again. Your child's death has changed many things about you and you will need time and patience to reacquaint yourself with the new person you have become!

Myth: Support groups are for weak people.

Truth: The truth is that the death of a child is the most isolating and lonely event in a human's life. Many grieving parents say that friends become strangers and strangers become friends. The reason for this is clear. How can anyone else possibly understand the depth of this pain if they have never experienced it before? An analogy I like to use is related to weight loss. Let's say I struggled with obesity all my life and finally made a decision to do whatever I needed to lose weight and become healthy again. Courageously, I check myself into a weight loss clinic. However, the mentor and counsellor assigned to help me through my struggle with weight is 110 lbs and a size three, and she has never been overweight a day in her life. How in the world is she going to understand your pain, your struggles and your fears? She never can. It is unlikely that you will even feel comfortable relating to that person. Support groups are a safe haven for parents to go and share the deepest of their pain with others who have experienced the same feelings. Many support groups are full of strong and compassionate people who are dedicated to helping newly bereaved parents find hope and peace in their life.

Myth: I am going crazy.
Truth: Every parent who has gone through the death of a child feels as if they are crazy. The vast array of emotions can overwhelm us. Many of us feel emotions we never knew we could feel. It is frightening and shocking. The usual routine of day-to-day life suddenly annoys us. We feel out of place even amongst the closest of family and friends. We cannot attend baby showers or birthday parties. We may feel too weak and drained to get out of bed in the morning. Once-enjoyed activities become dreaded tasks for us. Some parents are unable to perform at work, while others may become completely absorbed in their jobs as an attempt to escape the pain. Some parents express that the grief has become so unbearable, that they prayed God would take them while they sleep. It is a roller coaster ride. Some days we are able to laugh and feel joy again, while other days there seems a black cloud hanging over us the entire day. Who wouldn't feel crazy while undergoing all of these many emotions?

You aren't crazy. You are a grieving parent, simply missing what should have been in your life. Be patient and kind to yourself. While the longing for your child will never disappear, time grants us moments of peace in between the tidal waves of pain. Allow those peaceful moments to bring you closer to your child's love and the gifts they have left for you to discover.

By Joanne Cacciatore © 1998
from the book, 'Dear Cheyenne',
Mothers In Sympathy & Support (MISS),
1997,1998

Father's grief . . . when a baby dies

Information from SANDS, a support group for parents who experience miscarriage, stillbirth or neonatal death

Your baby has died
This is not how you expected this pregnancy to end. But it has. For both parents, this news initially evokes deep feelings of shock and confusion. In hospital, the nursing staff will assist with decisions you are required to make and discuss various options for creating memories and burial/cremation. These are also described in the SANDS book *Your baby has died . . .* (pp. 1-10).

Creating memories of your baby's short life is important. Many parents have found bathing and dressing their baby, taking footprints, handprints, a lock of hair, photos and holding their baby on more than one occasion to be a great source of comfort both at the time and in the years that follow. Many parents have later regretted not doing more at the time of their baby's delivery.

Bill reported that: 'Carrying her tiny coffin at the funeral remains a special memory for me.'

For Steve, baptising his tiny daughter, born after 19 weeks of pregnancy, 'reinforced her importance in our lives'.

Father's grief
As time passes those initial feelings of confusion and shock often turn to further confusion, distress, and sometimes rage.

After the loss of a baby, father's grief is often overlooked. Frequently it is assumed that fathers do not feel as much grief because, unlike

mothers, they have usually had little physical contact with the baby. Her feelings of loss are usually better accepted. Rob's experience is not uncommon: 'When I returned to work only 3 weeks after my baby son died, my boss enquired jovially, "Well, I expect you're over it now. How's Caroline?"'

But fathers do grieve
The loss of a baby is a life-changing event. Many change their values after this experience. Whether you had much contact or not, this baby was also your child – part of any dreams for the future

Sam commented: 'I had already imagined myself playing football with my boy in the park.'

Men and women typically express their grief differently. Our social practices make it very hard for fathers to express their grief openly. Men who cry or need to ask for help may be judged as weak, so many feel embarrassed to do so. This is less so for women. Similarly, while it is accepted women will talk through their problems and feelings, this is less accepted for men – although this is slowly changing.

Grief is a natural and healthy response to loss and is NOT managed by being ignored or avoided. For this reason alcohol and other substances are generally not helpful.

Many men feel much more emotion than they think they should show. Some try to block out these feelings by working harder or doing more – finding ways to stop themselves dwelling on sad thoughts. Unfortunately this will only postpone grieving.

Some fathers seem to suppress their grief until their partner is coping better. At this later stage it is more difficult to express their feelings openly as fewer supports are available. Reactions can then be complex, confused and prolonged. These may range from difficulties concentrating, or loss of interest in work, to over-involvement in work or excessive physical activity.

- Talking about your baby and shedding tears will assist your emotional healing. However if you don't normally cry you may not cry now. Express your feelings in a way that suits you.
- Try not to take on more work than you need over the coming months. Take time off or lighten your load as you need. Try to maintain a balance.
- Give yourself time for emotional healing.
- Reading about grief or talking to another parent may help you to accept your grief is normal.

Sometimes anger can add problems at this time, erupting when the slightest thing goes wrong.

- Express any anger, but direct it at things rather than people.
- Physical activity is often a good release.
- Do seek professional help if anger persists or things seem out of control.

A partner's grief

When a baby dies, a father may expect or be expected to support and console his partner. Some fathers may feel their own sadness must be suppressed in order to provide support. However sharing your sadness is a form of support and consolation.

Protecting your partner from the pain of her grief may add problems for you both. Coping with a partner's crying can trigger feelings of inadequacy and helplessness in a man, but distracting your partner from her grief can indicate that you want her grief over and done with. This may trigger misunderstanding and resentment.

Some couples expect that they can be sufficient support for each other. Although this may be so for a time, it is unlikely always to be the case. Many parents have found it helpful to seek support outside the family.

Not surprisingly, many of these reactions may affect the relationship between partners.

- Although it may be difficult, do try to be open with your partner about your feelings.
- Accept her feelings and reactions and avoid pushing her in any way.

Don't expect her to give you all the support you need right now. Find a friend or relative who has time to listen. Talking with other fathers who have had a similar loss can be very helpful.

You and your partner . . . helping each other

Those couples who can share their feelings and thoughts and support each other find this is a time that can enrich their relationship. This shared loss seems to bring them closer together, making it easier to bear.

- Be patient with each other and show your love in other ways, trusting that the loving and sexual feelings will return.

- Should any problems not improve with time, do seek professional help.

Occasionally, one partner may blame the other for the baby's death. This may stem from difficulties already existing in the relationship and will not help the situation.

- Professional help such as relationship counselling may provide valuable assistance if this is happening to you.

Recommendations

- Take time to make decisions – give yourself time to get accurate information and don't be afraid to ask questions.
- Acknowledge your grief – a special friend, work colleague or another person, especially one who has experienced loss, may provide valuable support.
- Express your grief in a way that suits you – many find it helpful to write down their feelings and thoughts in poetry, in songs or by spending time in the garden. Some cry a great deal, others very little or not at all.
- Be patient – with yourself and your partner. Remember that grief takes time.
- Accept your partner's grief – it will most likely be different from yours.
- Communicate with your partner – try to share your feelings and make joint decisions. Make time to do some special things together.
- Seek other resources – SANDS provides and can recommend more written material and also provides personal and group contact resources.
- Don't be afraid to ask for practical support – for childcare, domestic help or professional support.

In memory of

Callum Ian Murdoch Ray. SANDS (Vic) acknowledges the support and generosity of the family and friends of Callum's parents, Kath Murdoch and Stephen Ray, in the production of this information.

- The above is an extract from the SANDS (Vic) web site: www.sandsvic.org.au.

© SANDS (Victoria, Australia)

A death in the family

What to do

The emotional Issues

Death is a subject that none of us ever wants to think about, yet inevitably we will all have some contact with it in our lives. Our grandparents dealt with it far more often because it was a relatively more common event. For most of us it happens later in life and we don't have the chance to 'come to terms' with the idea, or indeed, learn how to grieve.

We normally feel grief after someone dies that we have known for some time. However it's clear that people who have lost babies, or had stillbirths or miscarriages, also suffer the same experiences, and need care, consideration and sometimes help dealing with their loss.

Occasionally the problems suffered go on for some time, and in some cases the family doctor can help, even if it's just someone to talk to. The doctor can also, if necessary, arrange for you to see a psychiatrist, or suggest other sources of help to you.

Whatever the case it is usually a very upsetting event making you feel that your whole world has been turned upside-down.

Children also feel grief and often great distress when someone close to them dies. A child's sense of time is different to that of an adult, and they may go through a mourning period quite quickly. In early school years, they may actually feel responsible for the death of a close relative, and need to be reassured. Young people may not want to upset grown-ups by speaking of their grief, because they feel they may be adding to the grown-up's sadness. It is important then not to overlook children when a member of the family has died, they may, for example, be included by helping with the funeral arrangements.

Having said all of this, there is no set pattern to grieving because we are all individuals. Different religions and cultures may also have different attitudes. Time is said to be a great healer, and people should be allowed the time that they need.

For most of us, despite all this, it's a part of life that we all go through, and usually does not require help from an outside source, or medical attention. For those of us that do have problems, help is available, not only from doctors, but from the organisations on pages 40-41.

The following is a brief summary of the steps that will need to be taken when you have to deal with the formalities following a death:

1. Inform the Doctor (unless the death occurs in hospital).

2. If the death is unexpected, and the doctor cannot issue a medical certificate, the Coroner must be told. In which case the Coroner will order a post-mortem and perhaps an inquest to determine the cause of death.

3. When the doctor (or hospital), is able to issue you with a Certificate of Cause of Death, contact a solicitor so that he can help you as much as possible.

4. Inform any relations who ought to be told.

5. If a British subject dies abroad, get in touch with the local British Embassy or the Consulate. The staff will advise you on the local regulations for registering a death, and will help you with arrangements for the funeral, or for bringing the body back to Britain.

6. A funeral director should then be approached (your solicitor may be able to recommend one to you if you wish).

7. Try to find if the deceased left a will to see if he or she requested burial or cremation, donation of organs etc.

8. Choose burial or cremation, as appropriate. (The funeral director will help in dealing with the formalities.)

9. Go to see the local Registrar of Deaths (taking the medical certificate with you) to report the death and to obtain the 'Green Certificate' from him which permits burial or cremation.

10. Give the 'Green Certificate' to the Funeral Director.

11. Discuss the funeral arrangements with the funeral director as follows:
- Where the deceased is to await funeral
- Possible embalming
- Which church and cemetery (or crematorium)
- The type of coffin
- The time and date of funeral
- The type of service (if required)
- Placing notices in newspapers
- Funeral cars
- Refreshment to mourners after the funeral
- Flowers

12. After the funeral, contact your solicitor again who will:
- Deal with the winding up of the estate.
- Claim national insurance benefits.
- Make arrangements for payment of the funeral directors.
- Consider if memorial service and/ or memorial stone is appropriate.

13. Reply to letters.

©1996-98 City 2000 (UK) Limited

Whose funeral is it?

Understanding and planning

There is quite enough pain around death and dying without adding more for the bereaved through anxiety about making suitable funeral arrangements. We leave our families with a burden when there is no understanding of what we should like to be done after our death or how it might be done. Discussion, planning, preparation is not macabre when we are alive, and when we are dead it's too late. Sudden, unexpected or premature death is the exception. Most people die nowadays at the end of a period of ill health or when they have reached an age at which death might be expected. Family members would feel more certain and comfortable and be able to express a clear choice to the funeral director, if there has been a degree of preparation. If we can begin to cope a little with the subject of death, which in a world of uncertain beliefs has become a taboo subject, then it makes it easier for others when it comes to start arranging the funeral. This is a time when we are often in a confused state, suffering from shock, despair, guilt, self-reproach or even disbelief.

So, tread carefully. There are really useful services to be bought from funeral directors, such as dealing with the statutory authorities, to save our energy, time and attention for personal details. But it seems we have to be alert enough to opt out of those parts of the package that we don't want or that seem inappropriate or downright distasteful – embalming for example.

The law offers more scope and more choices than most people think. The law protects and gives certain rights to people who choose to be buried or cremated without the rites of the Church of England, or indeed of any other church.

So, you do not need to have a funeral at all. If you do, it does not need to be in a licensed building – a small funeral could be at home, for example (unless you want an Anglican service in England). You

are not required to use a clergyman. You are not required to use an undertaker. By law, you are not required to use a coffin (but frequently local bylaws say you must if you want to enter an official cemetery or crematorium). Your burial may be on private land; you may be buried under a tree in your garden for example (although it is said to reduce the value of your property for your dependants; some say by £7,000 at least). In general avoid being within 50 metres of any well or borehole. Keep 10 metres from any standing or running water.

Bearing all this in mind may help with making some choices and in feeling some ownership of the funeral, although that is said with caution. A funeral must be about beginning to let go and not about achieving some private agenda or clinging to unfulfilled hopes for the person who has died.

Recommendations about planning and information are not an endorsement of pre-paid funeral plans, which get presented as a solution to part of the problem. While they are mechanisms for dealing with financial anxiety, they will become a reactionary force inhibiting change or a relook at the way we think about funerals. As it is a legal contract of service, with specified details, that is going to be entered into and signed up, maybe thirty years before it is acted upon, no one will give authority to change any of the details when the time comes. The proliferation of these schemes will actively prevent change and increase fossilisation of the service. Also, since they exclude disbursements – the fees and costs over which the funeral director has no responsibility (yet which can add another 30% to the bill), therefore he excludes them from the promised package – the family can still be in for a shock. And finally, as the supreme example of Pay Now Die Later, tying up all that money so far in advance has the industry laughing all the way to the bank.

Changes in consciousness might encourage people to plan in advance and might allow that not to be perceived as morbid, but helpful. The lady on the cheese stall in our weekly market, having seen my photograph in the local paper with a painted coffin, said: 'I think it's good; these things should be more in the open, more talked about. After all, just because I make a will, it doesn't mean I'm going to die.' A nice thought, but sadly, oh yes, you are. She is going to die and so am I, so we might as well recognise it.

• The above is an extract from *The Dead Good Funeral Guide*, produced by Engineers of the Imagination. See page 41 for address details.

© Engineers of the Imagination

The UK funeral market

Information from Engineers of the Imagination

In the UK the funeral market is currently estimated to be worth around £1 billion annually with around 640,000 funerals taking place each year. There are an estimated 4,000 funeral directors at present offering services but exact numbers are difficult to pinpoint as the profession is unregulated and anyone can enter it. About one-third of the market in 1987 was controlled by four organisations who have bought up and taken over many family firms, but their policies are to still trade under the well-known and local names, to give the illusion of a continuing, traditional service. This is shrewd marketing as many families keep a loyalty over the years to the same undertaker to arrange funerals within the extended family network when they arise. The annual survey of funeral costs in Britain showed in 1993 a burial cost on average £1,035 and cremation cost £830. There are great regional variations in cost. Burial in London and the South East is 50% more expensive than the North.

Researchers found that the price of an identical funeral varied by hundreds of pounds between different funeral directors in the same district, so it is worthwhile getting at least two quotations. One woman asked her MP to look into the matter when she was offered a discount if the account was settled before the funeral took place. 'Give them an inch, and they take a mile.'

Without question, we end up having booked their cars and drivers and bearers, having bought the coffin from their (inevitable) limited stock, having handed over the body of the deceased, probably to be embalmed, to be prepared for the coffin and dressed in the garments they have in stock. What if we don't like the style and design of any of the coffins or gowns in the catalogue? Who designed them? Who made the selection? How could we get anything different? We're pressed, through shortage of time, to make the best of it, yet why should we? As consumers, we are under no obligation to modify our wishes to meet the aspirations of traders in the field – and we have the Office of Fair Trading behind us all the way. Their concern is that information about options should be made available to members of the public and that nothing should stop people having them if that is what they want.

'He was marvellous – he took all the pressure off – all we had to do was pay the bill.'

'They bent over backwards to be kind. I relied completely on them.'

'I was asked all the time to decide on details immediately whereas I feel this could have been left until the following day when I was not so upset.'

Some decisions can wait till next day. Offers from the polished professional to 'see to everything' prey upon our vulnerability and our reticence. We may be concerned about the price yet in no way disrespectful in our attitude to the dead. Funeral directors have subtle ways of expressing their expectations that we will want only the best for our elderly relative and these are hard to refute when we feel guilty of neglecting them a little. Even harder is asking straightforward questions about how much it is all going to cost, and what the extras will be. Results of the Consumer Survey undertaken by the Office of Fair Trading in their report on funerals in 1987:

'3.26 Only 55% of people arranging a funeral in the sample had been given any information on the prices of different services available, and in more than half of those cases, where price information was given, there had been verbal discussion only.'

The funeral industry has invented elaborate rituals and seeks to persuade us that these are 'traditional'. Preying on our vulnerability, our anxiety, our guilt even, it is not difficult to see how a funeral can become manipulated into being a display of status. The professionals have to focus on the bereaved, since they seldom knew the person who has died. The family and friends at this time focus on the person who

has died. Here is potential conflict of interests and confusion around the focus of the funeral.

For example, there are two conflicting ways to read the image of a small bunch of wild flowers on the coffin, picked by a child. On the one hand it shows more about love and shared walks with a caring grand-parent than any tonnage of cello-phane hot-house bouquets from the professional florists. On the other hand, it appears they did not think much about grandad and were too mean to spend money on a decent show of flowers. It's hard to fight public taste and snobbery, especially at such a stressful time.

Debi, a friend, told how her father died a gentle, peaceful death at home after scarcely any illness, and the family kept the body at the house, and decided to prepare him for burial in his favourite gardening clothes – the old shoes, his corduroys, the cardigan mended on the elbow. That was more him than any stiff, dark suit – but why is 'keeping it in the family' disapproved of? It's personal, it's truthful, it's caring, it's 'hands-on', but it turns over less money on the balance sheet of the funeral industry – it jars against our culture of constant economic growth.

The growth of professional services and escalating costs is directly related to spiritual and social impoverishment. We live in a system where every time money changes hands we count ourselves richer, no matter what damage may be inherent in the transaction. The problem of capitalism, as Dr Tony Walter so succinctly puts it in his book *Funerals and how to improve them*, is not that funerals cost too much, but that they cost at all.

Production-line funerals are a prime example of this. At the end of the day, who are they for? A mother told us of her infant son's funeral, where she felt an outsider, not a participant. Many people we meet would like to see change. Some have faced a friend's funeral and not known what to do. Many have come out afterwards feeling the funeral did not represent what the person believed in life. We need a framework and resource material to hand, not strait-jackets.

• The above is an extract from *The Dead Good Funeral Guide*, produced by Engineers of the Imagination. See page 41 for address details.

© Engineers of the Imagination

Funeral plans

This estimate doesn't include the coffin, sir . . .
John Shaw on funeral cost shocks

Two shocks come with bereave-ment: the grief of death, and, a few weeks later, the bill. Coping with the emotional effects of one while trying to analyse unexpected charges in the other can be almost overwhelming for the bereaved.

The price of a funeral is made up of two key elements: basic costs and disbursements.

Basics are meant to cover an industry-agreed standard of funda-mental items: collection of the body and removal to a chapel of rest, a simple coffin and the hearse plus one car. The idea is that this represents a standard by which customers can understand costs and compare quotes.

But the annual survey of the Manchester Unity Friendly Society, one of the few organisations monitor-ing funeral costs in Britain, says this has now ended, and figures for a basic funeral are now 'meaningless'. The organisation has carried out surveys of the trade for the past 17 years.

Last year, for the first time, it detected two new trends: major elements were left out of the basic cost, and funeral and disbursement prices were consolidated into one figure.

But the estimated bill did not match up to the final total. The survey found 'under-estimates were considerable, often amounting to hundreds of pounds'. Philip Broeders, marketing director of the society, reveals that one funeral director in the Midlands and two in London did not include in their basic burial figure a coffin, hearse and car. Their interpretation of basic cost meant the funeral director's time, admin-istration, and use of the chapel of rest.

'Funeral directors may say they provide prices, but our research has shown that people are not being given all the information they need to make an informed judgment.

> **'You could be faced with a bill twice or even three times what you believed you were going to pay'**

'We believe if you haven't got the right information you could be faced with a bill twice or even three times what you believed you were going to pay.' The survey quotes the average cost of a burial at £1,657, up 8.8 per cent on 1996, and that of a cremation at £1,101, up 7.5 per cent.

Researchers found wider region-al variations. A burial in London cost £2,391 and a cremation £1,302. The price of the grave accounts for the higher funeral cost.

A burial elsewhere in the South East is much cheaper at £1,429 (cremation £1,020). But prices creep up in Yorkshire and Humberside (burial £1,632, cremation £1,195), the North West (£1,737 and £1,292), the North (£1,823 and £1,308) and Scotland (£1,912 and £1,131). In the South West burials average £1,402, cremations £915. The cheapest area is the East Midlands (£1,269 and £912).

• *Funeral Costs in Britain*, Manchester Unity Friendly Society. Free from Joan Loughlin, 0800 591 868.
© Telegraph Group Limited, London 1998

Cost of death can be exaggerated

By Sarah Hall

Dying is a costly business fraught with the risk of being financially exploited, it emerged yesterday.

The average cost of the most basic burial is now £1,657, rising to £2,391 in London and to £1,912 in Scotland, a new survey has revealed. Opting for a headstone can add £1,000 to the bill, the research, by the Manchester Unity Friendly Society, found.

The survey – based on random telephone enquiries to 100 undertakers in England, Scotland and Wales – also discovered the cost of dying varies enormously depending on where one happens to expire. The most thrifty should try to die in the East Midlands – where a basic burial will set you back £1,269 – or in Wales, where it costs £1,300. Prices have risen by 8.8 per cent in the two years since the last survey.

Regional variations can be partly explained by the differing cost of burial land, according to the society's spokesman, Paul Dwyer. The average plot costs £250-£500, but plots in one London borough can cost up to £3,000.

The end, two years ago, of local authority subsidies for cremations and burials has also caused greater variation, the society believes. Local authorities differ in the extent to which they adopt a commercial approach to the land – and in the degree to which they impose surcharges for burying non-residents. (Ipswich charges £292 for a burial plot for residents and £584 for non-residents, for instance, while one London borough's £505 resident's charge rises to £1,500 for those who did not live within its boundaries.)

But undertakers can also benefit from a general reluctance to quibble about funeral costs, the society

---

'There's still an old fashioned feeling . . . for many people organising a funeral that you can't or shouldn't mention the exact price. It might be regarded as tasteless'

---

believes. 'There's still an old-fashioned feeling . . . for many people organising a funeral that you can't or shouldn't mention the exact price. It might be regarded as tasteless,' Mr Dwyer said.

Dominic Maguire, of the National Association of Funeral Directors, whose members perform two-thirds of all funerals, said the survey was too small to be representative. He said: 'It's a fairly competitive market . . . and so anyone who hikes up charges is asking for trouble.'

Funeral fees

	Burials	Cremations
Average	£1,657	£1,102
London	£2,391	£1,302
Rest of SE	£1,429	£1,020
Scotland	£1,912	£1,131
Wales	£1,300	£1,004
Channel Isles	£1,572	£1,222
S West	£1,402	£915
E Anglia	£1,503	£931
E Midlands	£1,269	£912
W Midlands	£1,620	£935
Yorkshire & Humberside	£1,632	£1,195
N West	£1,737	£1,292
North	£1,823	£1,308

© *The Guardian*
March, 1998

Grave anxieties

When someone close to you dies, the last thing you want is hassle from the solicitor dealing with their will. Yet complaints of delay, overcharging and bad communication are rife. Sally Kinnes picks up the brief

When his mother-in-law died two years ago, Lawrence Curtis anticipated no problems with her will. 'There was no property, there were no complications and no dispute. Everything was to be divided between my wife, Sylvia, and her sister who get along famously,' says Curtis. 'All the money – which amounted to over £100,000 – was in the bank and the building society.'

Wills do not come much simpler than this. Even the solicitor assured them it wouldn't cost much. So they were horrified when his bill came to more than £2,200, based on an hourly rate of £105. 'The really objectionable thing was that he charged 1 per cent of the gross amount of the legacy on account of the complicated nature of the will,' says Curtis. 'It was ridiculous.'

On behalf of his wife, Curtis complained to the Office for the Supervision of Solicitors (OSS) who told him there was no case to answer. So he went to the Legal Services Ombudsman, who took a different view. 'She said OSS hadn't addressed my specific complaints, that it should have, and that as a result, I had been put to a great deal of work and inconvenience.' She recommended compensation of £200. 'It's a small victory,' says Curtis. 'I've just framed the cheque this morning.'

Curtis escaped lightly. Last year, OSS dealt with a probate case where the solicitor (now struck off), helped himself to £88,700 of the beneficiaries' estate. Administering wills is open to all kinds of temptations, and criticisms about how they are handled are the third most common complaint to the Ombudsman. Fees are one difficulty, delay another. 'Fairly simple things take months, even years,' says Nick O'Brien, legal adviser to the Ombudsman. 'Solicitors always seem to have something better to do.'

Coming into money isn't the pleasure it might be. Already distressed at their loss, those inheriting the estate (the beneficiaries) are frequently surprised to find themselves caught up in an expensive process over which they have little control. 'There are inherent disadvantages to beneficiaries in the legal system,' says O'Brien.

Solicitors can add to their bill 50 per cent 'profit mark-up' or 'uplift' for 'care and attention'

Beneficiaries, for instance, can complain about a solicitor, but they are not entitled to compensation. They can ask for a bill to be independently checked, but only in very specific circumstances. The trouble is, the beneficiaries aren't the solicitor's client, the executor is. Executors administer the will on the beneficiaries' behalf, but if the executor and solicitor are one and the same (and a solicitor is often named as one of the executors), this system breaks down. Many would say that it makes the solicitor unaccountable to anybody.

'I share the reservations of many complainants about the way in which the legal profession approaches probate work,' says the Ombudsman, Ann Abraham. 'Accountability is a particular problem when the solicitor is the sole executor and it's essential that beneficiaries are kept firmly at the centre of things and that OSS provides a way of finding redress when things go wrong.'

Complaints against solicitors have to go through three steps: the legal firm, then, if there's no satisfaction, OSS, and finally, if all else fails, the Ombudsman. The most controversial link in this chain is OSS. An enormous institution, which costs £12.5 million a year, it replaced the seriously flawed Solicitors' Complaints Bureau in 1996. But it's still run by the Law Society (the solicitors' professional body), is paid for by solicitors, and is even headed by a solicitor, director Peter Ross. Although its independence is now guaranteed, it has yet to shake off accusations of bias.

To take one example, concerning costs, solicitors can add to their bill 50 per cent 'profit mark-up' or 'uplift' for 'care and attention'. Most people reasonably assume that if you're paying around £200 an hour, care and attention should all be part of the service. Even the Law Society and OSS admit mark-up is complete nonsense. 'It probably is,' says OSS director Peter Ross. 'We're encouraging solicitors to avoid it.'

Despite this, when OSS checks bills for complainants, it still considers profit mark-up 'reasonable and fair'. In the case of a will, mark-up can be between 25 and 35 per cent, to which a 'value element' is then added on top. This is 0.5 per cent of the home, and 1 per cent of the rest of the estate, and if the solicitor is also the executor, these percentages are increased by 50 per cent – another reason, perhaps, not to make your solicitor your executor.

As long as it sides with solicitors over issues like this, OSS will have trouble winning consumer confidence. 'We're in a period of transition,' says Ross. 'We have made improvements, but we recognise we still have a long way to go.' Some people aren't prepared to wait. Unimpressed by the whole complaints procedure, a group of individuals has set up a pressure group to lobby for change. Known as CASIA (Campaign Against

Solicitors, Action for Independent Adjudication) it wants an end to self-regulation within the lifetime of this government, and a new body set up which has no connection with the Law Society.

There would be much less need for this, or any other sort of body, if solicitors didn't get themselves into such a mess with their clients in the first place. In 1997, one complaint was made for every three practising solicitors. Covering all legal services, lack of communication and failure to inform on costs were among the most frequent matters of concern.

The Law Society's defence of what might appear to be an intolerable level of customer dissatisfaction is that by their very nature client/solicitor relations cover areas of conflict and controversy where parties often emerge dissatisfied. However, while vague on fees, the Law Society does concede that solicitors are hopeless at handling complaints. 'When a client complains, criminal lawyers apply an almost criminal burden of proof. Civil lawyers apply a civil burden of proof,' says David McNeill, chief press officer for the Law Society of England and Wales. 'It's to do with their training.' Maybe, but it breeds a culture of suspicion, and an environment where lawyers are reluctant even to apologise lest there are legal implications to saying sorry.

In the face of such difficulties, CASIA is determined self-regulation should go. 'Our problem in the past has been the number of MPs who are solicitors or barristers themselves,' says vice chairman Tony Biles. Now this is a list which includes even the Prime Minister. He may be interested to know that the Ombudsman reckons the challenge for the law is to win public confidence, 'to construct what might fashionably be termed a "people's profession".' Maybe that'll get his attention.

Case by case

When Rosemary Catling's parents-in-law died, she and her husband administered their wills themselves. The wills were very straightforward, and it took them about three weeks. She would have done the same when her own father died in 1992, but although she had been named as one of the executors, her father's solicitor had been named as the other.

Nevertheless, she did much of the work herself. 'The will was very simple, and I was the sole beneficiary. Also, it was Christmas, and we couldn't contact the solicitor for a week. Then he said he wanted to come to the funeral, and had tea and cakes with us, more like a friend than a solicitor, really. Although he was my father's acquaintance, I don't think I had ever met him before.'

There was never any discussion about the solicitor's fee. 'I wrote to say I wanted to do as much as I could to cut down on the costs, and he wrote back quite a shirty letter. He was very high-handed about the whole thing.' But nothing prepared her for the size of the bill.

'He charged £2,000, which was 1 per cent of the estate, plus another £500 or so for selling the house. I paid in full. I suppose I should have made more of a fuss, but at the time, I wanted to get it finished with, and I didn't think I had any recourse. I thought that was what they could charge.'

Dr Elizabeth Gordon says: 'I think trustees are more dangerous than lawyers, but if your lawyer is your trustee, you are completely in their hands. Lawyers are a law unto themselves.' When her father died seven years ago, he left his money in trust to her and her children. He appointed as trustee of one trust, the senior partner at his solicitors. Trustees of the other were another solicitor in the same firm, and the articled clerk (trainee solicitor). His estate was valued at almost £1 million.

The cheapest option is to do it yourself. If the will is straightforward and uncontested, it's certainly worth considering

---

After her father's death, the senior partner and the articled clerk got married, and unbeknown to Gordon, the other solicitor ceased to be a trustee. Without consulting her, the husband and wife then appointed each other trustee of the trusts they looked after. Gordon now feels completely excluded from her own affairs.

Her father's house probated at £260,000 and in a sought-after area in the south of England, near a golf course, remains unsold after four years. The estate agents the solicitors claimed to have appointed to sell it say they received no such instruction. Meanwhile, fees for upkeep, a gardener and insurance come out of the trust, and Gordon worries about the depreciation value on an unlived-in house. She can't sell the house without the trustees' approval – 'they have unbelievable powers' – and she can't remove the trustees without going to court. 'I have to fight to get any accounts from them, but they charged £14,500 for the first year's work. I now have another solicitor looking into it. He thinks the whole thing stinks.'

Just who can you trust?

Solicitors charge large fees for administering estates, but it could be even worse if you go to a bank. Banks typically charge a hefty percentage of the estate, which is not necessarily a reflection of the work involved: £1 million left in the building society will be nothing like as complicated as £100,000 wrapped up in trusts and foreign property.

Banks also have a reputation for abruptly dropping estates which turn out to be less valuable than expected.

The cheapest option is to do it yourself. If the will is straightforward and uncontested, it's certainly worth considering. You'll need legal help to sell property or set up trusts, but the bulk of the work is a relatively straightforward question of form filling, asset valuing, and tax paying. In the first instance, contact your local probate registry, the number of which will be listed in the phone book.

© *The Guardian*
August, 1998

Green burial

The D-I-Y guide to law and practice

What happens to your mortal remains is up to you and the executors of your will. Choose executors prepared to obey the funeral instructions in your will. Nicholas Albery, editor of *The Natural Death Handbook* and a director of the UK educational charity the Natural Death Centre, prefers to leave his body to nature. In his will, he has specified that he wants to be buried on a piece of farmland that he and his wife were given as a wedding present, with no coffin, just wrapped in a sheet, and with an apple tree planted on top of him.

- Two-thirds of the people in the UK – such is their superstition about contemplating their own mortality – do not write a will.
- Leaving your body to science is an uncertain business – only non-cancerous, unautopsied, relatively whole bodies, within easy range of a medical school, are accepted.
- Anyone with green pretensions should think twice about cremation – 437,000 wooden coffins are wastefully burnt in the UK each year, polluting the atmosphere with dioxin, hydrochloric acid, hydrofluoric acid, sulphur dioxide and carbon dioxide.
- At least burial, even with a wooden coffin, locks the carbon underground and does not add to the greenhouse effect. And it helps protect land from being used by humans, thus saving it for wildlife.
- *The Natural Death Handbook* explains how families can go about organising cheap, green and 'D-I-Y' funerals without undertakers.
- Burials at sea: about 20 UK burials a year take place at sea. The licence is free, though the Ministry of Agriculture has produced a minefield of bureaucratic guidelines to discourage it.
- There are 85 or so nature reserve burial grounds in the UK already open, with 40 more applying for planning permission. At these woodland burial grounds, a tree is planted for each grave, which has no headstone, and, for those not using undertakers, cardboard coffins are obtainable, starting at £55, wooden coffins from £ 40 or lovely woollen shrouds at £120.
- The Natural Death Centre has researched the laws and regulations for the UK surrounding burial on farmland and in large private gardens – a recent case in England and a planning appeal in Scotland have confirmed that no planning permission is required for 'a limited number of unmarked and unfenced graves'. Anyone who nevertheless wishes to consult the Environment Agency (which encapsulates the former National Rivers Authority) and their local council environmental health department about possible pollution of water courses should go armed with chapter and verse on the regulations (available in the *Natural Death Handbook*), as local authorities find it hard to believe that the right to private burial has persisted from the days when Quakers often used to bury their relatives in the garden.
- Beware – garden burial can cause dissension if not all members of the family are in favour, and can reduce the value of the property.
- *The New Natural Death Handbook* (£ 11.65 incl. p&p) and various other books are available from The Natural Death Centre, 20 Heber Road, London NW2 6AA, UK (tel 0181 208 2853). *The New Natural Death Handbook* also covers Living Wills, Advance Funeral Wishes Forms, Death Plans, financial preparations for dying, caring for the dying, laying out the body, making a coffin, a good funeral guide to helpful professionals, bereavement, books and UK organisations.

• The above is an extract from the Natual Death Centre web site and can be accessed at www.global ideasbank.org/greenburial.html.

Co-op offers comfort and company with clubs for the bereaved

By Vanessa Thorpe

'When my husband died, some of my friends actually used to cross over to the other side of the road when they saw me coming,' said Sylvia Mosedale, a 61-year-old widow. 'People tend to shun you after a death.' After 45 years of marriage and lack of a friend's shoulder to cry on, Mrs Mosedale has turned to the comfort of a bereavement group, a newly formed, innovative organisation for those in mourning. Her group of 20 meets in Walsall, in the West Midlands, and is the blueprint for a series of similar groups to be set up across the country by the Co-op, Britain's biggest funeral director.

It is a simple idea, but a good one – and that, after all, is the way the Co-op made its name in the first place. Founded in Rochdale by 28 like-minded weavers, the co-operative movement now appears to be extending its famous 150-year-old 'cradle to the grave' principle beyond the grave itself. And the idea has caught on.

Co-operative societies in Wolverhampton, Rugeley and Kidderminster are to start groups of their own, while another Saturday group in the neighbouring West Midlands town of Brownhills has been running for some months.

In Walsall the group is led by Joan Rogers, a redoubtable 65-year-old who moved into the field after she took a counselling course. 'I had worked for the West Midlands Co-op all my life, and for the last 10 years I was with their funeral service. I took the course two years ago off my own bat,' she said. 'When I had finished, my manager, Diane Sysum, said: "We must make something of this".' Mrs Sysum was already looking for a way to offer free counselling to her customers after the funeral day because she knew how easily bereaved people can become isolated. 'I see it as part of the Co-op's philosophy,' she said.

'We run 4,000 funerals a year and this idea is not just a commercial gimmick. It is part of caring for the community.' The Walsall group started tentatively last year with only eight regular members, each of whom was first approached by phone. And the approach, it seems, is everything. Group member Pat Wright, who recently lost her husband after a long illness, explained: 'The doctor had asked me if I wanted to see a counsellor, but I didn't really like the idea back then. It was company that I wanted.' It's a view shared by Mrs Mosedale. 'After 45 years of marriage, I don't know where I would have been without this group,' she said.

The success of the group lies in the fact that the initial invitation to join comes from a funeral director who already has a practical relationship with the bereaved person. The offer is couched, too, in terms of friendship rather than of therapy.

'I do not much like the word "counselling",' said Mrs Rogers. 'I find it cold and think it puts people off. I spoke to this woman yesterday who said she thought it was wonderful that we still cared about her.' The ages in Mrs Rogers's group range from 54 to 83 and most of the members are women. There are, however, three elderly widowers among the regulars.

> **'After 45 years of marriage, I don't know where I would have been without this group'**

Eric, a 73-year-old former welder, has made good friends there. 'Dot, my wife, is still with me really – it would have been our golden wedding anniversary this year. So it is good to talk about her with other people; otherwise you would just sit and brood about things.' Richard, a 74-year-old retired engineer, agrees. 'I have no family, you see, so I was left alone when my wife died.' Yet for 67-year-old Iris, her recent bereavement is the last topic she wants to tackle with the group. 'There is not much I can say about it,' she said. 'I am a very private person and I have never been able to express my feelings about my husband.' The fact that many members choose to talk about everything but their loss confirms Mrs Rogers's belief that the group is really all about friendship.

Its main benefit is showing bereaved people that they are not alone.

'When somebody loses somebody they tend to think, "why me?" but when they come to these groups they realise it isn't just them,' she said. 'We don't usually have tears here, but that lady over there told us that when she tripped over going upstairs the other day at home she cried and cried, but now at least she has been able to come here and talk about it.' In 1828, Dr William King, a founding father of the co-op movement, wrote: 'Every year, the influence of Co-operation will spread with increasing energy; nor will any obstacle arrest its course till it has reached in splendid triumph the utmost limits of the habitable globe.' He would surely approve of the Walsall Co-op's attempts to extend a helping hand beyond the ultimate obstacle of death.

From the pulpit

No magic wand can ease the pain of loss. The Reverend Roy Cooper, a Methodist minister, explores the taboo subjects of death and bereavement with a Christian perspective

The knocking at the front door roused the woman from her sleep. She looked at the clock on the bedside locker and wondered who could be knocking at her door at 2.15am. Even as she made her way down the stairs the knocker was still rattling away.

The woman called out that she was coming and when she opened the hall door she was faced with a young policewoman.

With a soft and nervous voice the young PC asked the lady questions about her husband who was in hospital.

The lady confirmed his name and date of birth.

It seemed as though this line of questioning would keep going round in circles all night so the woman decided to break the circle.

'You are here to tell me that my husband is dead, aren't you?' With an almost audible sigh of relief, the young police officer nodded yes.

At that moment both women went into automatic pilot as they made their way in the police car to hospital.

I have a great deal of sympathy for that young police constable. It's never easy being the bearer of sad news, news that sends a tidal wave through the life of an individual and a family.

Yet one way or another all of you reading this article will be bereaved at some time in your life – it is simply all part of life experience.

You may feel that you are the only one to have been bereaved and in one very personal way, you are – but in another, you have joined a whole host of people, who just like you, are feeling the pain of loss.

If you have been bereaved, then only you understand the feeling that floods your mind when you hear the news – disbelief, shock, anger and pain are just some of the words which might come to mind.

But so often the initial reaction is a cold numbness, the feeling that you will wake up from this nightmare and all will be as it was before you went to sleep.

In recent days we have seen bereavement on national television in the faces of the family and friends of the three Quinn brothers, in the look of disbelief on the face of Mrs Kearney recounting the horrific death of her son.

The bewilderment of bereavement was evident in the face of a little child in the aftermath of a tidal wave in Papua New Guinea.

All we can do is 'feel' for them although we would love to take them into our arms and give them comfort.

While this might seem to be a solution, it's only a very short-term one.

What those who have been bereaved need is professional counselling.

Even though we all know that we are 'born to die', when death comes it usually catches us unawares.

It's going to happen to others but not us, we would like to believe.

Like the small boy who believes that all the grannies in the world, except his, are going to die. But then his dies and he doesn't know how to cope.

Some look to the Church thinking that they have some sort of magic wand which they can wave and all the pain and hurt and confusion will go away.

Christians are not exempted from bereavement. Even though those who die in faith know in the words of St Paul to be 'absent from the body' is to be 'present with the Lord', this does not make the ones left behind any less bereaved.

We are all human and grieve with the others who find themselves in the same situation.

But what they will discover is the comfort of their faith that the Lord is with them, touching them with human hands.

St Paul would also hope that out of their sorrow and stress they would have learned something of God's comfort and encouragement which they will pass on to those going through the same experience.

© Reverend Roy Cooper

Church acts over growing trend for secular funerals

By Victoria Combe,
Churches Correspondent

The Church is to campaign against the increasing commercialisation of the funeral business and promote the role of the parish church and local vicar in arranging funerals.

The General Synod will next month decide how to tackle the growing trend towards secular funerals arranged by conglomerates which reject or ignore the Christian teaching on death.

It will also debate during its four-day meeting in Westminster the value of lifelong celibacy as a 'Christian calling' and the role of church schools with a view to increasing their stake in education in the next Millennium.

Clare Short, secretary of state for international development, will answer questions from Synod members on what the Government is doing about international debt and Third World poverty.

A church report, *Good Funerals*, describes the transformation of the funeral industry over the last 30 years with many small family-owned firms being bought up by international companies which sell pre-paid funeral packages.

The Co-operative Society now holds a 25 per cent share of the market and the America-based Service Corporation International owns 14 per cent.

The Churches' Funerals Group believe that 70 per cent of the 600,000 funerals in England every year are conducted by Church of England clergy, but their role is under threat.

The Synod, which meets in Westminster, will debate proposals to improve the value of service offered by clergy including greater care for the bereaved and more attention to the content of the address and the worship.

The report recommends that the Church permit the 'ecologically virtuous' practice of recycling its burial grounds and extending churchyards to reduce the distance between the funeral service and place of burial.

Graveyards, it says, are a place where people come 'to mourn, to pray and find comfort' and churches should help the bereaved by making space for the burial of ashes as well as ministering at the graveside.

Tom Sutcliffe, a lay member of Southwark diocese, will ask Synod to support his motion which would encourage people to make preparations for their own death 'in co-operation with Christian ministers' and to take responsibility for the cost.

Cruse bereavement care

A support service for all bereaved people and those helping them

Cruse Bereavement Care has come a long way since it began caring for young widows and their children in 1959. Today it offers confidential counselling and support to all who are bereaved by death.

Cruse Bereavement Care is the largest organisation of its kind in the world, with almost 200 branches throughout the UK. The organisation has a volunteer workforce of over 6,400 of whom over 4,400 are bereavement counsellors, and last year it responded to almost 100,000 enquiries.

Cruse Bereavement Care continues to exist because there is a constant need for information on death and bereavement; a need for someone to listen when the grieving person needs to talk; a need for a safe place where feelings can be expressed; a need for assurance that what is going on is all part of grieving.

Many thousands of bereaved people receive face-to-face counselling free of charge and the opportunity for social support through Cruse Bereavement Care branches.

People can telephone or write to the Welfare Adviser for information and advice on practical issues relating to bereavement.

More than 100 books, booklets and pamphlets specifically for the bereaved and those who help them are available from the Cruse Bereavement Care mail order service. Publications for bereaved people include books about grief and recovery from loss, poetry books, practical information fact sheets, and fiction for children and adolescents. Resources for professionals are also available, including training manuals.

Cruse Bereavement Care offers external training for those whose work brings them into contact with the bereaved, such as nurses, doctors, clergy, welfare and personnel staff, funeral directors, life assurance representatives and many other professionals.

We also provide national and local training courses for bereavement counsellors and individually arranged training programmes for firms and organisations.

Cruse Bereavement Care has close links with other bereavement groups, statutory and voluntary organisations and works with Government departments on health and social issues which relate to bereaved people.

ADDITIONAL RESOURCES

Useful organisations and individuals. Abridged from *The Natural Death Handbook*.

AB Welfare & Wildlife Trust
7 Knox Road
Harrogate
North Yorkshire, HG1 3EF
Tel: 01423 530900
Advises dying and bereaved people on funerals and burials in any land anywhere in the country. Source for the Natural Death Centre and the general public of sound legal and ecological information.

Age Concern England (National Council on Ageing)
Astral House
1268 London Road
London, SW16 4ER
Tel: 0181 679 8000

Association of Burial Authorities
139 Kensington High Street
London, W8 6SU
Tel: 0171 937 0052
Fax: 0171 937 1393

BACUP (British Association of Cancer United Patients)
3 Bath Place
Rivington Street
London, EC2A 3JR
For information on any aspect of cancer call BACUP's Cancer Information Service staffed by specialist nurses tel: 0171 613 2121 or 0800 181199 Monday to Thursday 10am to 7pm; Friday 10am to 5.30pm

The Befriending Network
11 St Bernard's Road
Oxford, OX2 6EH
Tel: 01865 316200
Fax: 01235 768867; or London 0181 208 2853 or 0181 208 0670
Volunteers who can visit those with critical illnesses for two to three hours per week.

Bristol Cancer Help Centre
Grove House
Cornwallis Grove
Clifton
Bristol, BS8 4PG
Tel: 0117 980 9500

British Humanist Association
47 Theobald's Road
London, WC1X 8SP
Tel: 0171 430 0908 or
0990 168122
Can provide officiant (normally charging £50-£60) for non-religious funeral.

British Organ Donor Society (BODY)
Balsham
Cambridge, CB1 6DL
Tel: 01223 893636

The Buddhist Hospice Trust
5 Grayswood Point
Norley Vale, Roehampton
London, SW15 4BT
Tel: c/o Ray Wills 0181 789 6170
Volunteers in its Ananda Network are prepared to sit with and befriend the terminally ill.

CancerLink
11-21 Northdown Street
London, N1 9BN
Tel: 0171 833 2818
Freephone cancer information helpline 0800 132905

Child Bereavement Trust
Harleyford Estate
Henley Road
Marlow, SL7 2DX
Tel: 01628 48801

Child Death Helpline
c/o Bereavement Services Department
Great Ormond Street Hospital
London
Freephone helpline 0800 282986 staffed every night 7 to 10pm and Wednesday mornings 10am to 1pm; administration 0171 813 8551 or 0151 252 5391.

The Compassionate Friends
53 North Street
Bristol, BS3 1EN
Tel 0117 953 9639 helpline
Tel 0117 966 5202 admin
Befriends bereaved adults.

The Cot Death Helpline
Tel: 0171 235 1721 24-hour manned helpline.

Cremation Society of Great Britain
2nd Floor, Brecon House
16/16a Albion Place
Maidstone, ME14 5DZ
Tel: 01622 688292

Cruse Bereavement Care
Cruse House
126 Sheen Road
Richmond
Surrey, TW9 1UR
Tel: 0181 940 4818
Bereavement counsellor available on 0181 332 7227 weekdays 9.30am to 5pm.
Founded in 1959, Cruse Bereavement Care is a national charity offering help to all who are bereaved – young and old, men women and children, wherever they live in the United Kingdom. They produce a wide range of leaflets, books and information.

Cruse Bereavement Care (Scotland)
33/35 Boswall Parkway
Edinburgh, EH5 2BR
Offers counselling for those bereaved, to enable them to go on in a hopeful and positive way, providing advice and social groups. Also provides training from the Scottish Heaquarters for those who work with death and dying. The training is offered in the form of one-day seminars/workshops, 60-hour foundation courses, intensive 30-hour courses for those with prior learning. Also specialises in working with children.

Elisabeth Kübler-Ross Foundation
Panther House
38 Mount Pleasant
London, WC1H 0AP
In the USA the Foundation's phone number is 001 703 396 3441

Engineers of the Imagination
Welfare State International
The Ellers
Ulverston
Cumbria, LA12 0AA
Tel: 01229 581127
Produces a series of books on rights of passage including *The Dead Good Funeral Guide* (£9.50 plus £1.50 postage and packing). Books are available by mail order from the above address.

Federation of British Cremation Authorities
41 Salisbury Road
Carshalton
Surrey, SM5 3HA
Tel: 0181 669 4521

The Foundation for the Study of Infant Deaths
14 Halkin Street
London, SW1X 8QB
Tel: 0171 235 0965
24-hour staffed helpline for families and professionals: 0171 235 1721

The Funeral Ombudsman
31 Southampton Row
London, WC1B 5HJ
Tel: 0171 430 1112
For complaints about Co-op and non-NAFD funeral directors.

The Hospice Information Service
at St Christopher's Hospice
51-59 Lawrie Park Road
Sydenham
London, SE26 6DZ
Tel: 0181 778 9252

Ian Rennie Hospice at Home
93 Western Road
Tring
Hertfordshire, HP23 4BN
Tel: 01442 890222
Trained nurses provide free full nursing breaks for carers.

Institute of Burial and Cremation Administration
One The Terrace
City of London Cemetery
Manor Park
London, E12 5DO
Tel & Fax 0181 989 9496
Publishes the excellent *Charter for the Bereaved* (the full 72-page reference copy costs £25).

Jewish Bereavement Counselling Service
PO Box 6748
London, N3 3BX
Tel: 0181 349 0839 answerphone

Lesbian and Gay Bereavement Project
Vaughan M. Williams Centre
Colindale Hospital
London, NW9 5GJ
Tel: 0181 200 0511 (admin)
Runs a helpline on 0181 455 8894.

London Association of Bereavement Services
356 Holloway Road
London, N7 6PN
Tel: 0171 700 8134

Memorials by Artists
Snape Priory
Saxmundham
Suffolk, IP17 1SA
Tel: 01728 688 934
Nation-wide service to put people in touch with designer-carvers who make individual memorials.

Miscarriage Association
Clayton Hospital
Northgate
Wakefield, WF1 3JF
Tel: 01924 200799
Support and information.

National Association of Bereavement Services
20 Norton Folgate
London, E1 6DB
Tel: 0171 247 1080 referrals
0171 247 0617 admin

National Association of Widows
54-57 Allison Street
Digbeth
Birmingham, B5 5TH
Tel: 0121 643 8348

Natural Death Centre
20 Heber Road
London, NW2 6AA
Tel: 0181 208 2853

Probate Registry
Personal Applications Dept
2nd Floor, Principal Registry
Family Division, Somerset House
Strand, London, WC2R 1LP
Tel: 0171 936 6983 answerphone
or 0171 936 6939

Rigpa
330 Caledonian Road
London, N1 1BB
Tel: 0171 700 0185
Tibetan Buddhist centre founded by Sogyal Rinpoche. Runs courses on death and dying.

Shadow of Suicide (SOS)
53 North Street
Bristol, BS3 1EN
Tel: 0117 953 9639
Support for families where a child (of any age including adult) has died by suicide.

Caroline Sherwood
6 St George's Court
The Archers Way
Glastonbury, BA6 9JB
Tel: 01458 835432
Offers counselling and teaching by phone or mail for people wanting help with fear of death, bereavement and associated issues.

The Starlight Foundation
8A Bloomsbury Square
London, WC1A 2LP
Tel: 0171 430 1642
Attempts to grant the wishes of chronically and terminally ill children.

The Stillbirth and Neonatal Death Society (SANDS)
28 Portland Place
London, W1N 4DE
Tel: 0171 436 5881

Support After Murder or Manslaughter (SAMM)
Cranmer House
39 Brixton Road
London, SW9 6DZ
Tel: 0171 735 3838

Terrence Higgins Trust
52-54 Grays Inn Road
London, WC1X 8JU
Tel: 0171 831 0330
A registered charity to inform, advise and help on AIDS and HIV infection.

Twins and Multiple Births Association – Bereavement Support Group
PO Box 30, Little Sutton
South Wirral, L66 1TH
Tel: 0151 348 0020

INDEX

Independence Web News

Back | Forward | Home | Reload | Images | Open | Print | Find | Stop

Live Home Page | Search | Computer | Support | System

The Internet has been likened to shopping in a supermarket without aisles. The press of a button on a Web browser can bring up thousands of sites but working your way through them to find what you want can involve long and frustrating on-line searches.

And unfortunately many sites contain inaccurate, misleading or heavily biased information. Our researchers have therefore undertaken an extensive analysis to bring you a selection of quality Web site addresses.

* * * * *

London Bereavement Network (LBN)
www.bereavement.demon.co.uk/
There are a vast number of resources and a wealth of information on the Internet relating to bereavement. This site provide numerous such sites through its links page. Well worth a look.

The Natural Death Centre
http://newciv.org/worldtrans/naturaldeath.html
A charity whose aim is to promote dignified death. An impressive site with a vast amount of information about death and dying and including their Good Funeral Guide which gives practical information about arranging a cheap but dignified funeral with details of recommended funeral directors in London and elsewhere.

Terrence Higgins Trust
www.tht.org.uk/pubs
Terrence Higgins Trust is a major, London based, UK resource for people with AIDS or HIV and their carers.

Hospices on the Net in UK & Ireland
www.digiserve.com/hauraki/hospice.htm
A page containing links to all the hospices currently with Internet presence in the UK and Ireland, a total of sixteen at the last count.

The WEBster: Death, Dying and Grief Guide
www.katsden.com/death/index.html
A massive list of links to resources covering every aspect of death, dying and bereavement. This is a very large page indeed and takes a good while to load but is well worth the wait.

WidowNet
www.fortnet.org/WidowNet
A bereavement site 'by and for widows and widowers'. Quite an interesting site with many good links. However, it is not always easy to find what you want as it is not well categorised.

ACKNOWLEDGEMENTS

The publisher is grateful for permission to reproduce the following material.

While every care has been taken to trace and acknowledge copyright, the publisher tenders its apology for any accidental infringement or where copyright has proved untraceable. The publisher would be pleased to come to a suitable arrangement in any such case with the rightful owner.

Chapter One: Coming To Terms With Death

Coping with bereavement, © The Terrence Higgins Trust, 1996-1998, *Grieving*, © The Prince & Princess of Wales Hospice, *Drawn to the light*, © The Guardian, June 1998, *Widows urged to talk about death*, © The Irish Times, July 1998, *Attitude to death in Ireland is praised*, © The Irish Times, July 1998, *Coping with the loss of a loved one*, © Yours Magazine, September 1998, *Cruse youth line*, © Cruse Bereavement Care, *About bereavement*, © London Bereavement Network (LBN), *Death and dying*, © Death & Dying, 1997, 1998, *Studies show that pets can help people cope with bereavement*, © The Scotsman, September 1998, *Pain of loss as a part of death*, © The Herald, April 1998, *When you lose someone close*, © The Guardian, September 1997, *Grief and the adolescent*, © TAG: Teen Age Grief, Inc., *Death in the family*, © Royal College of Psychiatrists, October 1996, *Death story wins child book prize*, © The Guardian, July 1998, *Bereavement*, © ChildLine, *Student counselling*, © Royal Holloway University of London, *Coping with pet loss*, © British

Small Animal Veterinary Association (BSAVA), *How do you live with the death of a child?*, © The Independent, August 1998, *Common myths about the death of your child*, © Mothers In Sympathy & Support (MISS), 1997-1998, *Fathers grief . . . when a baby dies*, © SANDS (Vic)

Chapter Two: Dealing With the Formalities

A death in the family, © 1996-1998 City 2000 (UK) Limited, *Whose funeral is it?*, © Engineers of the Imagination, *The UK funeral market*, © Engineers of the Imagination, *Funeral plans*, © Telegraph Group Limited, London 1998, *Cost of a death can be exaggerated*, © The Guardian, March 1998, *Grave anxieties*, © The Guardian, August 1998, *Green burial*, © The Natural Death Centre, October 1998, *Co-op offers comfort and company with clubs for the bereaved*, © The Independent, July 1998, *From the pulpit*, © Reverend Roy Cooper, *Church acts over growing trend for secular funerals*, © Telegraph Group Limited, London 1998, *Cruse bereavement care*, © Cruse Bereavement Care.

Photographs and illustrations:

Pages 1, 6, 8, 12, 14, 15, 20, 22, 30, 31, 33, 36, 38: Pumpkin House.

Craig Donnellan
Cambridge
January, 1999